Grassland & Woodland in Spring

Reader's Digest
Wildlife Watch

Grassland & Woodland in Spring

Published by
The Reader's Digest Association Limited
London • New York • Sydney • Montreal

contents

Wildlife habitats and havens

12 The downs – chalk, grass and flowers

18 Hedgerows in the landscape

24 Hardy hawthorn

28 The oak wood

34 Glorious bluebell groves

40 Northumberland's nature trails

Woodland watch

86 The badger

92 The family life of foxes

98 The great spotted woodpecker

104 Recognising finches

111 Centipedes and millipedes

115 Orange-tip butterfly

117 Anemones and relatives

122 Wild violets

126 Index

128 Acknowledgments

Animals and plants in focus

Grassland watch

48 The rabbit

54 The bank vole

60 The barn owl

66 Recognising buntings

71 The dung beetle

75 Wild grasses

80 Golden dandelions

Spring is the season of light. Early mornings can still be cold, with frost crisping the grass in the blue shadow of the hedgerow. But with the dawn of each new day the sun climbs a little higher in the sky and, as the grey winter landscape soaks up the light, it begins to glow with colour and life.

At first the difference is hard to pin down. The thorn hedges are bare and so are the deciduous oak, ash, hazel and beech trees in the woodlands. But there is something about the ends of the twigs. All winter they have looked thin, mean and almost dead, but now they appear plumper, richer and alive. Their buds are swelling and soon they will burst into new leaf. Meanwhile, down on the ground, woodland flowers bloom in the spring sunshine, before the leaves unfurling above them block out the light.

The first cuckoo of spring is usually heard by the third week in April, but for small birds the call is a warning rather than a welcome sign.

In March and April, male and female brown hares indulge in wild chases over open grassland, and may spar with each other like boxers.

The well-named early purple orchid flowers among bluebells in May, making a splash of deep colour among the shimmering drifts of blue.

Ancient turf

Over recent decades, much of the old grassland that once provided pasture and winter fodder for cattle and sheep has been ploughed up, reseeded with a few high-protein grasses such as ryegrass and laced with nitrogen-rich fertiliser. It may still be grass, but in spring the difference is plain to see. Where the reseeded pastures are a deep, plain green, the ancient grasslands sparkle with low-growing, flowering herbs and grassland butterflies such as the chalkhill blue dance among the wild grasses.

Luckily, many areas of ancient grassland survive, particularly in the uplands and on the steeper slopes of chalk downland (see pages 12–17). These grasslands were cultivated many centuries ago, and in some places, such as parts of the Wiltshire Downs, you can still see traces of abandoned fields dating back to the Iron Age. Their survival shows that the land has not been ploughed since, and if you walk across them you may be walking on turf that is over two thousand years old.

River valleys are richly fertile and tend to be ploughed for arable crops. Despite this, some patches of ancient grassland survive, often in winter-flooded riverside fields that are too wet to be cultivated in the spring. Such places are traditionally used as haymeadows and support a rich flora that reaches its peak in early summer. But a few of these meadows – most famously Magdalen College Meadow in Oxford – bloom in late April with the strangely sculptured, chequered purple, or occasionally white, flowers of the snakeshead fritillary. In a good fritillary year the meadow is suffused with a wine-stained haze of nodding blooms, but by the end of May the vision has faded, like spring itself, into the deep green of summer.

Sheets of colour

In the deciduous forests, and especially oak woodlands (see pages 28–33), spring is a critical time. For a few weeks the woodland floor beneath the bare branches is flooded with light, but once the leaves expand to their full size they intercept most of the sunlight's energy, diverting it to the trees. So the plants of the woodland floor have to move fast. They are well prepared, having spent the previous summer

The green shoots of dog's mercury can cover the ground in oak woods. Places where it is found in the open are often the sites of vanished woodlands.

The common blue butterfly lays its eggs on grassland plants such as bird's-foot trefoil, a habit that allows it to live throughout much of Britain.

A tall relative of the primrose, the cowslip often forms large colonies on old, undisturbed chalk and limestone grasslands.

8

absorbing nutrients and storing them in thick roots and bulbs. When the spring sunshine starts to warm the earth, they are primed to make the most of it.

The earliest flower to appear in the woods is the pure white snowdrop. It often blooms in February, when there are so few insects about that it rarely gets pollinated. This means that it cannot set seed and it spreads by division of its bulbs instead. Growing numbers of wild snowdrop colonies are expanding through damp woodlands, particularly in Shropshire and Somerset.

It may be that the snowdrop was introduced from a warmer climate several centuries ago but there are no such doubts about the wild daffodil, an authentic native that flowers a month later when the first insect pollinators are on the wing. Although now rare, it still forms colonies in old woodlands, which often overflow onto grasslands. It shares its insect visitors with the far more widespread lesser celandine, a relative of the buttercup that opens its flowers in bright sunlight and closes them again as the light fades. The celandine is

soon followed by the delicate wood anemone (see pages 117–121) and then by the most celebrated woodland flower of all, the bluebell (see pages 34–39).

Between them, these plants transform many woodland floors into sheets of colour as they flower and set seed. But by the end of spring the trees have spread their leaves and, starved of light, the colourful flowers wither away and die, leaving the green foliage to gather what light it can.

Fresh foliage

The beech woods of the Chiltern Hills in central southern England cast such a dense shade in summer that few plants can survive at ground level. Even in spring the woodland floor is mostly carpeted with dead leaves. But the trees themselves are glorious, with layer upon layer of fresh, newly unfurled leaves of radiant emerald green.

Ash opens its delicate green leaves a little later, and never casts such a dense shade as beech. So unlike beech forests, the ash woodlands of northern and western limestone soils have a rich ground flora. One of the finest is Colt Park Wood in the northern Pennines, where the trees sprout from cracks – or grikes – eroded by rainwater in exposed limestone 'pavement'. In spring the smaller cracks are filled with the flowers of lime-loving plants such as crane's-bills.

The green woodpecker feeds its young mainly on ants, so it is often to be seen on grassland, where it uses its extremely long, sticky tongue to scoop up the insects from their anthills.

When they first open, the tender young leaves of beech trees are vivid green and fringed with silky hairs. The leaves turn darker green in summer.

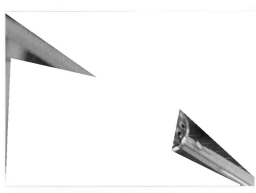

Although it still breeds in both woods and grassland, laying its eggs on primroses and cowslips, the Duke of Burgundy has become a very scarce butterfly in Britain due to intensive farming practices, the decline in coppicing old woodland and the depredations of rabbits, which destroy the caterpillars' foodplants.

Woodland music

Deciduous woodlands are full of birdsong in spring, when year-round residents such as the robin and song thrush are joined by migrants such as the chiffchaff and blackcap, all at their most vocal as rival males compete for breeding territory. The chiffchaff's song is a monotonous repetition of its name – and therefore one of the most easily identified of all birdsongs, after the cuckoo – but the blackcap sings with a rich, pure, full-throated warble that rivals that of the most famous singer of all, the nightingale.

Nightingales are among the most elusive of woodland birds, being both secretive and well camouflaged. The whole character of the nightingale seems to be concentrated in its wonderfully powerful and inventive song. When they are newly arrived in southern England from Africa the males sing only by day, claiming their territories with a shorter, stripped-down version of their song. But as May gives way to June they start to sing by night as well, using their full repertoire to fill the night air with haunting beauty.

Living boundaries

Nightingales frequent dense scrub as well as woodland and often sing from deep within thick, old hedgerows. These living boundaries (see pages 18–23) are like elongated extensions of the woods, and the oldest of them are rich in plants that may include many spring-flowering woodland species such as primrose and bluebell. Some of the most ancient hedges may even be remnants of the original wildwood, left between fields that were cleared for agriculture hundreds, if not thousands, of years ago. Most hedges, however, are far more recent, having been planted in the 18th and 19th centuries to subdivide large fields into smaller ones.

It is estimated that in the three decades between 1945 and 1975 – the main period of hedgerow removal – some 226,000km (140,000 miles) of hedges were torn out. Yet roughly 772,000km (480,000 miles) remain in the British Isles, including many of the biggest, oldest and most valuable to wildlife.

They make ideal nesting sites for seed-eating birds such as finches (see pages 104–110), which feed on adjacent fields, and the banks at their roots are often riddled with the burrows of rabbits (see pages 48–53), whose destructive activities on arable land have prompted the removal of many a redundant hedge. The hedgerow flowers also attract a variety of spring butterflies, which are often able to breed on the native plants growing at the hedge bottom. Since many hedges divide vast tracts of cultivated land, sown with alien plants that native insects cannot eat – or find deadly owing to the use of pesticides – the hedgerows are probably vital to the survival of farmland insects and insect-eating birds.

The delicate lilac cuckoo flower blooms in damp meadows, hedgerows and ditches. It is one of the main foodplants of the orange-tip butterfly.

Sometimes known as the maybug, the clumsy cockchafer emerges in swarms in mid-spring, after spending years living underground as a root-eating larva.

The tiny yet ferocious weasel hunts throughout the winter on grasslands and in woods, and bears its young in spring when prey is easier to find.

Wildlife habitats and havens

- The downs – chalk, grass and flowers
- Hedgerows in the landscape
- Hardy hawthorn
- The oak wood
- Glorious bluebell groves
- Northumberland's nature trails

The downs – chalk, grass and flowers

The ancient pasture of the chalk downs is one of Britain's finest grassland habitats. Rich in colourful wild flowers, the turf comes alive with butterflies and breeding birds from early spring.

Chalk is one of the most easily identified rocks in Britain, thanks to the familiarity of the spectacular white cliffs of Dover. Together with Beachy Head in East Sussex, Lulworth Cove in Dorset and Flamborough Head in Yorkshire, these cliffs mark the ends of a chalk outcrop that underlies much of southern and eastern

England. In many areas north of the River Thames, the chalk underlies flat lowlands covered by extensive layers of boulder clay, which was dumped during the last ice age. But in the south particularly, the chalk forms the rolling hills that we call the downs.

Almost pure calcium carbonate, chalk leaves very little mineral residue as it is gradually dissolved by rainwater. The soils that result

In many areas, grazing sheep have been replaced by rabbits. Both help to prevent the grassland being invaded by scrub and reverting to woodland, but too many of either can create problems through overgrazing.

are therefore very chalky and quite shallow, especially on the steeper slopes. Despite this, the natural vegetation of the downs is woodland, and large areas of downland are still covered with forests of beech and oak. However, great tracts were cleared of trees by

farmers in prehistoric times, and ever since then much of the land has been used for growing farm crops and grazing livestock.

Springy turf

The remains of prehistoric and medieval arable fields can still be seen on the downs, covered by resilient, spongy turf created by centuries of grazing by sheep. From about 600 years ago, rabbits colonised the downs and, under the two-pronged assault of sheep and rabbits, the downs remained mostly under grass until early in the 20th century.

Large tracts were ploughed up during the two World Wars, but grazing kept the rest open until the 1950s, when myxomatosis wiped out most of the rabbit population. Sheep-grazing had already greatly declined, and the loss of the rabbits allowed scrub to invade the downland.

▼ Box Hill on the North Downs is one of the most accessible areas of chalk downland in southern England. Despite suffering from the pressure of many visitors, it still represents some of the best chalk grassland in Britain.

DOWNLAND FLOWERS

In parts of the downs where the ancient pasture still survives, grasses and other herbs create a living mosaic which may contain more than 30 plant species in each square metre (yard). The plants are low-growing species that can survive constant trampling and grazing. The ox-eye daisy flowers throughout the year and mouse-ear hawkweed opens its bright yellow flowers between May and October. It is often accompanied by rough hawkbit and autumnal hawkbit, the yellow flowers of which carpet huge areas of grassland in late summer and are often mistaken for dandelions. Bird's-foot trefoil,

kidney vetch and horseshoe vetch add more yellow to the carpet in spring and summer. At a few sites, mainly in the Chilterns and Cotswolds, the pasqueflower opens its stunning deep purple blooms from late April to May, often in time for Easter. A range of purple, pink and blue flowers appear later in the year. They include the delicate harebell and its sturdier relative the clustered bellflower, the knapweeds and scabious, and marjoram, autumn gentian and the dwarf (or stemless) thistle. The latter has been dubbed the picnic thistle because it always seems to grow on the ideal picnic spot.

▶ The flowers of the ox-eye daisy tend to be smaller on downland than elsewhere – the exposed conditions do not favour big showy blooms.

▼ Flowering from April, the pasqueflower is surely the most beautiful of downland flowers, and one of the rarest.

▲ Clustered bellflower blooms at the height of summer. Its blue flowers are very attractive to pollinating insects such as hover flies and butterflies.

▶ Most people recognise dwarf thistle by its sharp spines, but in midsummer it also produces attractive red-purple flowers.

The Conservation Corps – the forerunner of the British Trust for Conservation Volunteers (BTCV) – set to work clearing the encroaching hawthorn, buckthorn and dogwood scrub but it was a losing battle and much of the grassland reverted to woodland. Elsewhere the economics of modern agriculture prompted farmers to plough up the ancient

grassland and use the land to grow barley and other crops. Nevertheless, many areas of ancient grassland survive on Salisbury Plain and the neighbouring Wiltshire Downs, in the Chilterns and on the North and South Downs. The grasses are often taller than they used to be and the plant variety is somewhat reduced, but the downs still support a wonderful array of plant and animal life.

Deep roots

Chalk is a porous rock, draining water very quickly, so many downland plants have drought-resistant characteristics. These include small leaves with hairy or waxy coatings. The leaves of many of the grasses are tightly rolled to cut down water loss and some of the other plants have extremely long roots

The rich turf of the chalk downs was created by centuries of grazing by sheep as well as rabbits, and appropriate levels of grazing still play a vital part in downland management.

that can reach moisture lying deep in the chalk. The roots of salad burnet and lady's bedstraw, for example, commonly reach 60cm (2ft) below the surface, so the plant is actually bigger below the ground than above it.

The main chalkland grasses are sheep's fescue and the very similar red fescue. They have very narrow, tightly rolled, almost needle-like leaves. Other downland grasses include meadow oat grass, crested hair grass and the daintily branched quaking grass or totter grass. You may also find several small sedges, which can be identified by their triangular stems.

In the less heavily grazed areas, the smaller grasses and herbs are commonly swamped by upright brome grass and tor grass. The latter is a tough grass that spreads quickly because few animals eat it, and its bright green or yellowish green colour is clearly visible from a distance.

Grasshoppers and ants

The abundant grass and other vegetation of the downs feeds a tremendous variety of insects, including six species of grasshopper. Their buzzing songs fill the air on sunny days throughout the spring and summer. The song of each grasshopper has its own

Grasshoppers such as this stripe-winged grasshopper are abundant in areas of chalk grassland, especially in southern England. On sunny days the songs of the males fill the air and it is often possible to discern the sounds of several different species at once.

particular pitch and rhythm, and the males use it to attract females of the same species. Most grasshoppers inhabit any type of grassland, but the stripe-winged and rufous grasshoppers have a strong preference for chalk and limestone hills.

The most numerous insects on the downs are ants. Mounds created by the yellowish coloured meadow ant are sometimes so abundant that they make walking difficult. Densities of 5500 nests per hectare (13,600 per acre) have been recorded on some parts of the North Downs and, with up to 70,000 ants in each mound, it is clear they play a major role in downland ecology. The ants feed on insects and mites in the soil, along with a sweet fluid called honeydew obtained from aphids living on plant roots. Wild thyme and common rock-rose frequently grow on ant mounds.

Downland birds

The most familiar bird of downland is probably the skylark, although numbers have declined dramatically

ORCHIDS

Most of our native orchids prefer lime-rich soils, and several species occur regularly on the downs. Although not as dazzling as tropical orchids, some of them – such as the aptly named bee orchid and monkey orchid – are very striking. Others, including the musk orchid and the frog orchid, have much less obvious greenish flowers. Most species flower in late spring and early summer, but you must wait until August or even later to find the elegant, fragrant spiral flower spikes of autumn lady's-tresses.

▲ Burnt orchid gets its name from the scorched appearance of its flower buds. It has a very patchy distribution but is abundant in some places, such as parts of the Wiltshire Downs.

▲ The discovery of a bee orchid is a highlight of any visit to chalk downland. As the plant's name suggests, the flowers bear a distinct resemblance to bumble-bees, but insect pollination is rare in Britain where the plant is almost always self-pollinated.

▲ Extremely rare in Britain, the monkey orchid favours sites where woodland and scrub have encroached on open downland.

▶ The pyramidal orchid is quite widespread and common. Its flower spikes are conical in outline in their early stages, but they gradually expand and round out with age.

in recent decades, especially in areas where intensive farming has destroyed much of its food supply. The male performs a continuous warbling, whistling, trilling song high above his nest site, often rising to 100m (over 300ft) and singing for three minutes or more. Skylarks are often confused with meadow pipits, also found on downland, but the pipit is smaller with a more slender beak, no sign of a crest on its head and a relatively longer tail.

Scrub song

Both the skylark and meadow pipit nest on the ground in open areas of grassland, whereas the yellowhammer prefers the scrubbier parts of the downs, where it nests low down in bushes and trills its familiar '*little-bit-of-bread-and-no-cheeeeeese*' song from the upper branches. In spring and summer these downland residents are joined by visitors including the whinchat and

the wheatear. Small birds such as these have to watch out for kestrels, which also snatch voles and insects as they hover over the grassland. This common falcon is occasionally joined by the closely related, but much scarcer, hobby.

▼ The many small mammals and birds that live on downland attract a variety of predators. The most conspicuous of these hunters is the kestrel, which is easily identified by the way it hovers over the grassy slopes watching for the telltale movements of prey.

▲ Several species of ants live on chalk downland, building large mounds in areas where the ground has not been ploughed for centuries. The presence of many mounds is an indication of an undisturbed site, rich in wildlife.

DOWNLAND SNAILS

The lime-rich soil of chalk downland is ideal for snails, which need calcium carbonate to make their shells. The largest species is the Roman or edible snail. Its thick, creamy white shell, often with brown bands, is most often found on the North Downs and in the Chilterns. The dark-lipped and white-lipped banded snails are both very

▲ Roman snails are so called because they were eaten by Roman settlers in Britain. They have become common in places and are often seen moving around in the open in overcast or rainy weather.

common. Their shells are usually yellow with brown bands, but the pattern varies and many snails have no bands at all. Heavily banded specimens are most common in scrubby, shady areas where they are well camouflaged. Lightly banded or unbanded snails occur mainly in the more open, well-lit areas.

Keep an eye open for the strongly ribbed, conical shell of the round-mouthed snail. Unlike any other downland snail, it can close its shell with a horny plate called an operculum.

Snails of various kinds are attacked by the larvae of glow-worms, and it is always worth examining the shells for these diminutive predators.

▲ If it is in danger of drying out, the round-mouthed snail can withdraw into its shell and seal itself in with a tough, waterproof trapdoor.

▲ Famous for their lofty songflights, skylarks raise their young in mossy nests on the ground. The chicks respond to danger by sitting very still, relying on their speckled and streaky plumage for camouflage.

▶ The song of the yellowhammer is a familiar sound on chalk downland in spring, when the birds nest in areas of hawthorn scrub and other patches of cover. In winter, they form small flocks that range nomadically across areas of farmland.

The downland was created by grazing, and the best way to save the remaining fragments of this once extensive habitat is to keep grazing them. Sheep are used on many downland nature reserves, and by careful management it is possible to maintain a full range of the plants and animals that make downland such a magical part of our wildlife heritage.

The corn bunting's curious key-jangling song is not heard as often as it once was due to the massive decline of the species.

Rolling chalk downlands support a host of wild flowers that, in turn, attract a wide variety of butterflies and birds.

WILDLIFE WATCH

Where can I explore chalk downland?

● **Box Hill**
This popular site on the North Downs in Surrey has open downland and areas of mature woodland, including yew with an understorey of box. Grassland plants include yellow-rattle, basil-thyme and marjoram; butterflies include silver-spotted skipper and chalkhill blue. The Roman snail is common here.

● **Beachy Head**
A well-known beauty spot, Beachy Head is located where the South Downs meet the sea in East Sussex. Butterflies to be seen here include chalkhill blue and grizzled skipper; flowers include small hare's-ear (one of only two sites in Britain), bastard toadflax and several species of orchid.

● **Butser Hill**
Excellent chalk downland in Hampshire, Butser Hill supports numerous blue butterflies and marbled whites. Flowers include greater knapweed, squinancywort and several species of orchid.

● **Pulpit Hill and Ivinghoe Beacon**
This superb chalk downland is located in the Chiltern Hills of Buckinghamshire.

Marbled white, chalkhill blue and small blue butterflies are to be seen on Pulpit Hill, and Ivinghoe supports Duke of Burgundy and brown argus butterflies as well as pasqueflower.

● **Therfield Heath**
Steep downland near Royston, Hertfordshire, Therfield Heath is one of the best sites in Britain for pasqueflower. It also supports spotted cat's-ear, bee and fragrant orchids, bastard toadflax and wild candytuft.

● **Devil's Dyke**
Although it is not really downland, this interesting stretch of chalk grassland near Newmarket in Cambridgeshire is well worth exploring at all times of year.

● **Compton Down**
Situated on the Isle of Wight where the chalk ends in the famous Needles, Compton Down offers superb scenery. Flowers include bee and pyramidal orchids and yellow-wort; butterflies include chalkhill and adonis blues, marbled white and dark green fritillary.

BUTTERFLIES AND MOTHS

Three groups of butterflies – the skippers, the browns and the blues – are particularly associated with chalk grasslands. Although less common than they were 50 years ago when they flew up in clouds as people walked over the downs, they are still plentiful in places.

The skippers are all small butterflies, named for their darting and dancing flight close to the ground. Seven of Britain's eight species breed on the downs. The silver-spotted, large, small, Essex and Lulworth skippers are largely orange, and they are collectively known as golden skippers. Their caterpillars all feed on grasses. The dingy skipper is dark brown, the grizzled skipper is blackish and white; their caterpillars eat low-growing plants.

The browns, typified by the meadow brown and the small heath, can be recognised by the small eye spots near the wing tips, and often all around the wing margins. As their name suggests, they are mostly brown, but the marbled white is a striking exception. In the caterpillar stage, they all feed on grasses.

The brightest of the downland butterflies are the blues, although only the males of most species are really blue. Four species breed on the downs, plus the brown argus, which belongs to the same group but has only a few bluish hairs on its body. The most widespread species is the common blue, which occurs in all kinds of grassy places. The chalkhill, adonis and small blues are confined to chalk and limestone

grassland. All their caterpillars feed on low-growing members of the pea family.

Keep an eye open for the dark green fritillary, one of the largest of downland butterflies, and also for the Duke of Burgundy. Resembling a small fritillary, this butterfly likes sunny, sheltered spots and has benefited from scrub-invasion of the hillsides. Its caterpillars feed mainly on cowslips.

Walking through taller grasses usually disturbs a lot of small brownish moths that quickly settle again and disappear from sight. These are various species of grass moths. With their wings wrapped tightly around their bodies, they blend extremely well with the grass stems, but close examination reveals exquisite patterns that give the moths their

Dark green fritillaries are common on some parts of the downs, but they can be difficult to see because they are very active and fast-flying on sunny days.

alternative name of grass veneers.

Three species of burnet moth feed freely on the flower heads of knapweeds and scabious during the summer – the six-spot burnet, the five-spot burnet and the narrow-bordered five-spot burnet. Their bold black and red colours warn of their unpleasant and potentially dangerous nature, for these insects contain cyanide in their bodies. Few birds dare to attack them. Their caterpillars feed on bird's-foot trefoil and other members of the pea family. The papery cocoons of the six-spot and narrow-bordered five-spot burnets are spun high on grass stems in early summer, but those of the five-spot burnet are usually well hidden

among low vegetation. The cocoons of the drinker moth are also attached to grass stems, but they are much larger and more fibrous than the burnet cocoons. This moth gets its name from the caterpillar's habit of drinking dew. The furry brown adult moths fly mainly at night.

▼ The adonis blue has two broods each year, so the male's dazzling blue upperwings grace the downland scene in May and June, and again in late summer. The female has mainly brown upperwings.

▲ Dingy skipper adults are on the wing between May and June. After mating, the female will lay her eggs on bird's-foot trefoil.

▶ The long, hairy caterpillar of the drinker moth emerges from hibernation in April.

Hedgerows in the landscape

Studying the structure and layout of a locality's hedges reveals much about its heritage, since the hedgerow bridges the gap between natural and human history.

There are two ways to look at a hedge. You could view it as a fence made of bushes that provides useful food and shelter for wildlife in a landscape of open fields. Or, perhaps less obviously, you could see it as an elongated piece of living history – archaeology with leaves.

Hedgerows have marked the divisions of the British farming landscape for centuries – in some areas they may be as old as farming itself. Although most hedges are dominated by one or two shrubs – mainly hawthorn and blackthorn – ancient hedges can be as individual as parish churches.

In the sandy Breckland district of East Anglia, there are contorted hedges of Scots pine planted as windbreaks. On the other side of England in Cornwall, hedges of gorse stand on banks made of boulders covered with turf. Some hedges carry fully grown oak or ash trees at regular intervals; others line brooks or sunken lanes, with aprons of bramble and tapestries of primroses and other woodland flowers at their bases.

Many people will remember the old elm hedgerows, with their proud billowy trees cresting the landscape. Elm suckers still sprout to form shrubs in the hedgerow, but most of the mature trees fell victim to Dutch elm disease in the 1970s. Their blackening stumps can still be found half-hidden in some hedges.

Ancient boundaries

Many people assume that all hedges were planted by landowners within the past 250 years, as part of the enclosure movement, which divided up the open landscape of medieval agriculture. But although many hedges were planted during this period, others – nearly always the most interesting ones – are much, much older.

A genuinely old hedge can be distinguished from a more recently planted one by the species found in it. Young hedges are nearly always composed of one or two quick-growing shrubs that were deliberately planted. Other shrubs colonise the hedge naturally over time, perhaps from berries dropped by songbirds or nuts buried by jays or squirrels. Hazel, holly and maple normally take a long time to become established in a hedge, and so their presence can be taken as a sign of age. If you find species such as the small-leaved lime or wild service tree, the hedge was probably not planted at all and may, in fact, be the outline of a former wood, sometimes known as a 'ghost hedge'.

Young hedges usually follow straight lines around square fields, as in eastern Leicestershire. The purpose of such hedges was straightforward: to keep livestock in, or out of, a field. Older hedgerows are hardly ever straight; instead, they

◀ There are few better ways of deterring straying livestock – or people for that matter – than by topping a stone wall with a hedgerow of impenetrable, prickly holly.

▶ The hedgerows of Devon are renowned for the luxuriant growth of plants that they encourage. Here, the hedgerow flowers include perforate St John's-wort and wild basil.

Blackthorn was widely planted in hedgerows for its stout, stockproof thorns. It flowers in early spring, turning whole hedges white with blossom.

whole kingdoms. An example is Offa's Dyke, the old border between England and Wales. Many of these banks were crested by hedges – a fact proven both by the age of existing hedges and from the detailed descriptions in Saxon estate charters. It is in some of these documents that hedges are first described as 'hegerœwe' or hedgerows, meaning hedges with rows of trees. This distinction between a hedge and a hedgerow has all but disappeared today.

We do not know if these ancient hedges were planted or whether they sprang up naturally, although both origins are possible. Hedges were useful enough to be deliberately planted. Apart from their primary functions as boundaries and barriers, they were sources of firewood, nuts and berries, and fodder for animals.

The farming landscape of this period was not as densely hedged as that of 50 years ago, when Britain probably had more hedges than it ever had before. The original hedges must have been quite imposing, however, standing on steep banks, often with dry ditches in front and perhaps studded with ivy-covered stumps and pollards, which are hammer-headed trees regularly cut above cattle-browsing height for firewood. The discovery of such a hedge on your own patch, even if it is now in tatters, can bring you as close to your local history as any guided tour of ruined architecture.

tend to weave about and turn corners, often following natural landscape features such as brooks or contour lines. They can be very thick and may contain mature trees, or at least their stumps.

The original purpose of many old hedges was not purely agricultural. An old hedge often marks a boundary, such as that of a parish or a long-established estate. Originally, the word 'hedge' just meant boundary. It is derived from the old English word 'haga' or 'hege',

which seems to have referred to a hedge bank rather than the hedge itself. This is significant, since old England was a country crosshatched with earth banks of all shapes and sizes, from the walls around parks and villages to the boundary banks of parishes and properties. On the largest scale, earth banks were even used to demarcate

Primroses and violets are basically woodland flowers, but they can often be seen blossoming beneath old hedges in spring.

Some of the finest examples of hedgerow networks can be found among the rolling hills of Exmoor. Many of the hedges here date back hundreds of years.

HEDGEROW MANAGEMENT

In the past, farm hedges were valuable and therefore usually well maintained. There were no artificial fertilisers, so farmers needed livestock to provide manure for their crops. Before the invention of barbed-wire fencing, a well-maintained stockproof hedge was one of the best ways of keeping the animals and crops apart.

How a hedge was pruned and managed varied from place to place. In many areas, including the Midlands, hedges were made into stockproof barriers by a process called laying. A portion of each old stem is retained, but partly cut through with a billhook. The stem is then bent over and secured at one end with a stake. The next stem is then 'laid' over the first, and

Nowadays, hedges are regularly cut back with flail cutters. This should be done in winter to minimise disruption to wildlife and avoid harming nesting birds.

so on. The result is a barrier of bent branches which soon sprout vertically to form a thick hedge. The beauty of the system is that the hedge remains stockproof throughout, and sprouts new growth much faster than a newly planted one.

There are many regional variations in hedge laying, as there are in the hedger's tools. Fortunately, the technique has enjoyed a revival, and today the benefits of the hedger's art can be appreciated throughout the country.

▲ Periodically, hedgerows need to undergo laying if they are to survive long term without becoming 'leggy' and full of gaps at ground level. Hedge laying is an ancient and skilled art, but it is still practised in many parts of Britain.

▶ In the first season after laying, the hedgerow begins to thicken up. By year three, all signs of the laying process will have disappeared behind the tangled layers of new growth. Laid hedges are good for nesting birds.

In some regions, such as Kent and Sussex, hedges were traditionally coppiced or lopped. This produced a less regular hedge, with a tight row of separate bushes with large trunks or stools.

Before the development of power tools, many hedges were maintained by workmen using clippers. Laid hedges were normally clipped into a

box shape, rather like the privet hedges of suburban gardens. Repeated clipping, however, tended to produce an A-shaped hedge with a narrow top.

Today most hedges are not so much trimmed as thrashed with a tractor-driven flail cutter. A recently flailed hedge looks a sorry sight with its raw, broken branches, but the method can maintain a dense hedge.

▲ Opportunistic animals such as grey squirrels make the most of overgrown hedgerows, treating them as extensions of the woodlands.

Overgrown hedges

Where hedges have become redundant they are all too often grubbed out, or so ruthlessly cut back that they decay into isolated bushes punctuating barbed wire fences. But if they are left to their own devices, hedgerows quickly grow rampant, and many are fast turning into narrow woods. Identifying such overgrown hedges is not always straightforward, however. In the Sussex Weald, many fields are divided by woody strips which were never planted, but are remnants of natural woodland. They are neither hedges nor woods, so they have a name of their own: they are called 'shaws'.

Wildlife refuges

Today, hedges have acquired a new value as refuges and 'green corridors' for wildlife. From the point of view of a fox or a bank vole, a hedge is a narrow shrubbery extending across dangerous open ground, providing cover and food and linking larger refuges such as woodlands. A big neglected hedge can be a prime habitat in its own right, and may even have a diverse woodland flora at its roots. As agriculture becomes more intensive, creating increasingly hostile environments for wildlife, hedges become all the more important as providers of food and shelter.

▲ Severely cut hedgerows alongside main roads allow wild flowers, such as red campion and cow parsley, to flourish.

◄ Hedges are important nesting habitats for a wide variety of birds, such as this blackbird. If the hedges vanish, the birds often disappear too.

During the past few years, local authorities have come to recognise the value of older hedges, both as historical artefacts and as wildlife refuges. They now have the power to list important hedges – generally older and more species-rich ones – and impose fines for damaging them.

This change of heart has come too late for regions that have lost most of their ancient hedges, but it is still welcome. It offers new hope for the historic hedge that separates a parish from its neighbour, and places like the Welsh Borders or the Blackmore Vale in Dorset where hedges still dominate the landscape.

The giant beech hedge at Meikleour, Perthshire, is over 25m (80ft) high. It keeps its old leaves throughout the winter, and they begin to fall only when the new growth pushes through in spring.

WILDLIFE WATCH

How can I learn more about hedgerows?

● Hedges tend to be taken for granted, but they are among the glories of lowland landscapes. Moreover, they are easy to study and usually accessible along country lanes and bridlepaths.

● Courses dealing with the practical management of hedgerows – including the techniques of hedge laying – operate at field centres across the country. Contact your local Wildlife Trust or the Field Studies Council at: FSC, Central Services, Preston Montford, Montford Bridge, Shrewsbury, SY4 1HW (telephone 01743 850380), or visit their website at www.field-studies-council.org

● You can discover the approximate age of a hedge by counting the number of constituent shrubs growing in a stretch 30m (100ft) long. Climbers such as traveller's joy and ivy should not be included. The total equates roughly to the hedge's age in centuries, so a hedge with five species was probably planted 500 years ago, in Tudor times. This rule of thumb is known as Hooper's Rule after Dr Max Hooper, the biologist who discovered it. The method needs to be used with caution and common sense, discounting obvious anomalies. Results can also be affected by the fact that there are typically fewer hedgerow species in the north than in southern England and Wales, and more species tend to grow on limestone than clay.

● If you try out Hooper's Rule in a country parish near you, you will find a hidden pattern beginning to emerge as you plot hedge lines on a map. The older hedgerows will probably line ancient tracks and lanes, and the oldest of all may lie on the parish boundary itself. By looking up old maps in the local library, you can begin to flesh out these bare bones of history and appreciate what lies behind this seemingly random pattern of hedges, fields and lanes. To a skilled interpreter, these boundaries are as full of meaning and history as the ruins of any medieval castle or ancient hillfort.

● In Oxfordshire there are some wonderful old hedges standing on broad grass verges. These once marked the boundaries of Saxon 'hundreds', units of land that have been redundant for almost a millennium.

● Beech hedges were often planted to mark the boundaries of farms or parishes. Although these are nowadays often neglected, they can still be found growing in long lines of tall, mature trees on parts of Exmoor, in central Wales, the New Forest and Scotland.

● The finest examples of the patchwork system of hedgerows can be found in the West Country. The South Hams in south Devon and parts of Exmoor offer some of the best opportunities to see this classic English landscape.

● Limited resources and manpower mean that today most hedgerows have to be cut mechanically, using a flail cutter. This operation is best done in the dead of winter, after the berries and nuts have been exploited by birds and mammals and before the buds have begun to burst into leaf in spring. Cutting at any other time of year can make hedges less likely to regenerate, and may be harmful to wildlife.

The field and hedgerow system remains an integral part of the Dorset landscape.

Hardy hawthorn

For centuries the hawthorn has been valued for its ability to form a stockproof hedge, but its thorny branches, blossom and berries also protect and feed a whole range of wildlife.

Few trees are as deeply enshrined in rural tradition as the hawthorn. Mankind has enjoyed a fruitful association with the tree since prehistory, and our knowledge of the species has become enriched with tales of magic and mystery. Historically, the flowering of the hawthorn has always been associated with the month of May, giving the tree its popular name. After the long, colourless months of winter, the appearance of its blossom in spring heralded the seasons of abundance that were to follow. In pagan times the blossom was associated with fertility and many country traditions have their roots in this belief.

However, it is not only people that have a close relationship with the hawthorn. As one of the most numerous and widespread trees in the countryside, it provides a vital source of food and shelter for wildlife.

Sharp defences
Hawthorn grows vigorously, its thorny branches creating an almost impenetrable barrier when cut back and trained to form a hedge. In this traditional craft, called laying, waste growth is cut away to leave a row of upright stems, called 'pleachers', which are partly cut at an angle near their bases and bent over. The new growth they produce eventually forms a dense hedge. As a result, the hawthorn has been valued throughout history, and has become an integral part of the landscape.

Its jumbled and spiky branches were probably first used by nomadic herdsmen to protect their livestock from the wolves and bears that roamed the forests of ancient Britain. With the advent of farming and agriculture, the hawthorn became even more established. During the land enclosures of the 18th and 19th centuries, mile upon mile of hawthorn hedges were

▶ The dense, prickly branches of a hawthorn may conceal the delicate, purse-shaped nest of a long-tailed tit, protecting the eggs and young from predators.

▼ Wood mice use their sharp claws to scramble through the hawthorn bushes in search of food – young shoots in the spring, berries in the autumn.

▶ The hawthorn blossom that opens in spring turns whole bushes – and sometimes entire hedgerows – white with its massed frothy flowers.

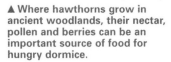

▲ Where hawthorns grow in ancient woodlands, their nectar, pollen and berries can be an important source of food for hungry dormice.

COMMON HAWTHORN FACT FILE

The common hawthorn is a beautiful tree that is distantly related to the rose. In spring, it produces a mass of small, heavily scented flowers, which in autumn give rise to the characteristic clusters of bright red 'hips', or 'haws', that give the tree its common name. It is often confused with another native British member of the group, the Midland hawthorn.

● NAMES
Common names: common hawthorn, English hawthorn, May tree, whitethorn, quickthorn, 'bread-and-cheese' tree
Scientific name: *Crataegus monogyna*

● HABITAT
Rapid coloniser of dry ground and free-draining soils, particularly limestone; common in hedgerows, scrub, open woodlands and parks

● DISTRIBUTION
Throughout most of Britain and Ireland; less common in Scotland

● HEIGHT
Up to 14m (50ft), sometimes more; girth of trunk can reach over 45cm (18in)

● LIFESPAN
At least 400 years, probably more

● BARK
In saplings, bark is grey and relatively smooth; becomes gnarled in older trees and splits into regular-shaped brown plates with deep fissures and furrows

● LEAVES
Arise singly on alternate sides of stem; small, up to 4.5cm (1¾in); deeply lobed

● TWIGS
Well armed with short, sharp thorns

● FLOWERS
White or pale pink, heavily scented, borne in clusters of 10–18; appear May–June; individual flowers 8–15mm (⅜–⅝in) in diameter with single style (upper part of female reproductive organ)

● FRUITS
Also called haws; bright red, oval, 8–10mm (⅜in) long; each contains a single seed

● USES
Hard-wearing, dense timber; burns well and makes good charcoal; bark was used to dye wool black; leaves and fruits edible although not palatable

The outline is broadly spreading.

Gnarled bark can appear like twisted rope.

Each red, fleshy 'haw' contains a single seed.

Paired, leaf-like stipules are located at base of each leaf.

Single leaves with deeply divided lobes grow on each side of the stem.

The clusters of flowers are white or pale pink.

Despite their inviting appearance, hawthorn berries are woody and pithy and not very palatable to humans. However, a wide variety of birds, mammals and insects feast on them.

MIDLAND HAWTHORN

Less abundant and much less widespread than the common hawthorn, Midland hawthorn, Crataegus laevigata, occurs mainly in the Midlands and south-east England, and usually as a tree rather than a hedge. Since this tree is tolerant of shade, it is often found as a dense understorey shrub in woodland on heavy soils.

The two species can be distinguished by their leaves, flowers and fruits. The leaves of Midland hawthorn have just three shallow lobes and are shinier above, and the mainly white flowers have a stronger, unpleasant scent. The flowers have two or three styles, and the fruits bear two or three seeds. By comparison, each flower of common hawthorn has just one style and the fruit contains a single seed.

Sometimes known as the woodland hawthorn, Midland hawthorn crosses freely with its common cousin, producing decorative hybrids that are often found in parks and gardens. It is also planted as cover for gamebirds.

planted to keep livestock in the newly created fields and away from tempting crops.

So much was invested in planting these prickly barriers that their maintenance was of the utmost importance. Hedges were regularly laid to maintain their vigour and keep them stockproof. Hedge-laying is still employed by some landowners, but the hawthorn hedge has been largely replaced by modern alternatives such as barbed wire and strand netting. As a result, many hawthorn hedgerows are now derelict and exist only as lines of trees.

Long-lived trees

These hawthorn trees surprise some people. The widespread use of hawthorn as a hedging plant means that it is often

▲ The normally ground-dwelling bank vole is often lured up into hawthorn bushes by their nutritious berries and may collect the seeds as a winter food store.

regarded as a small woody shrub, rather than a tree. In fact, it is a slow-growing species that, given the right location and enough time, is capable of becoming a sizable tree over 14m (50ft) tall. However, its branches are very dense and typically spread to form an extremely thick canopy, which creates the deceptive appearance of a compact tree, as wide as it is high.

Individual hawthorn trees are known to have lived for 400 years, and it is possible that this hardy species is capable of living even longer.

HOLY THORN

The hawthorn plays the main role in the legend of the Glastonbury thorn, which concerns the arrival of the Christian faith to Celtic Britain. Joseph of Arimathea – the owner of the tomb in which Jesus was laid – is said to have visited Glastonbury. On arrival, he rested on his hawthorn staff at the top of Wearyall Hill. The staff took root and became a blossoming hawthorn tree. From then on the tree was known as the Glastonbury thorn and was said to flower only on Christmas day to celebrate the birth of Christ.

Legend maintains that the Glastonbury thorn was still alive in the mid-17th century, and it is said that James I paid large sums for cuttings of the tree to ensure its survival. The association of the winter-flowering thorn tree with royalty is preserved to this day and the Queen is presented with its flowering twigs each Christmas.

Modern cultivars known as Glastonbury thorn, *Crataegus monogyna* 'Biflora', are today available from nurseries. They may even be descended from the original tree.

One tree in central Norfolk is believed to be at least 700 years old.

Seductive scent

The early appearance of the hawthorn's nectar-laden flowers provides a valuable source of food for a variety of insects that are active early in the year. On warm spring evenings the heavily scented flowers are alive with bees, beetles, flies and moths. Lappet, lackey and oak eggar moths lay their eggs on its leaves, so that their plump caterpillars can feed on its vigorous foliage. Smaller

moths, such as the common pug, seek cover on the tree's fissured bark and also lay their eggs on its leaves.

Insects are not the only creatures attracted to the hawthorn in spring. Dormice, newly emerged from winter hibernation, travel long distances along hedgerows to feed on the pollen and nectar in the blossom. The fresh young shoots provide an important food for browsing

▼ The superb camouflage of the lappet moth allows it to rest unseen on dead beech leaves, but as a caterpillar it often feeds on hawthorn foliage.

▲ A number of moth species use hawthorn leaves as a foodplant for their caterpillars, including the often seen yellowtail moth.

◄ A buff-tip moth may use a hawthorn as a daytime perch, disguised by its resemblance to a lichen-covered twig that has snapped off at both ends.

◄ The spiny twigs and dense foliage of a mature hawthorn bush can provide well-protected nesting sites for birds such as woodpigeons.

▼ With its massive, conical bill, the hawfinch is one of the few birds capable of cracking the hard hawthorn seeds found inside the soft red berries.

roe deer and, in the past, the young leaves were eaten by people too. This gave rise to the oddest of the species' country names – the 'bread-and-cheese' tree.

The hawthorn's dense, tangled crown and almost impenetrable mass of thorns also provides excellent cover for nesting birds, from finches to magpies. The thickest bushes may shelter the tiny, lichen-covered nests of the charming long-tailed tit.

Later in the year the hawthorn is transformed by

a rich display of bright red berries. These are one of the most important sources of food for birds and attract a variety of migrant thrushes, such as redwings and fieldfares, as well as resident species including mistle thrushes, blackbirds, robins, woodpigeons and the scarce and elusive hawfinch. Pugnacious mistle thrushes will often guard individual bushes and spend hours chasing off flocks of redwings and fieldfares that try to poach their precious berries. The

hawthorn seeds are left undamaged by their passage through the birds' guts, making the birds valuable agents of dispersal.

Even those berries that drop to the ground are not wasted, being gathered up by hungry bank voles, wood mice

and squirrels. They eat the soft flesh straight away, but when the berries are abundant, voles may accumulate vast hoards of the seeds beneath log piles to see them through the hard winter months, before the May blossom signals the arrival of spring once again.

WILDLIFE WATCH

Where can I see hawthorn?

● Common hawthorn is widespread throughout the British Isles and found almost everywhere except on mountain tops and waterlogged ground.

● The best displays are often found on chalk downland slopes, where, unless checked, the bushes can form almost impenetrable scrub.

● Hawthorn is a common plant of hedgerows throughout Britain, and is often the dominant species. It responds well to sympathetic cutting and laying, and is an extremely important plant for wildlife.

As an isolated specimen, the hawthorn often grows into a stately, well-rounded tree, which is smothered with foamy white blossom in spring.

The oak wood

The spreading canopy of oak trees shelters a rich tapestry of life that changes with the seasons.

The oak tree, with its sturdy trunk, massive twisting branches and thickly furrowed bark, is one of the most recognisable of all our native trees. Its deeply lobed leaves and nut-like acorns in their neat cups are unmistakable at close range, but even at a distance the tree is instantly identifiable by the majestic character of its spreading crown.

Oaks began to appear in the forests and woodlands of Britain soon after the last ice age drew to a close, around 10,000 years ago. As Europe warmed up and the ice retreated northward, pioneer plants resembling the annual weeds of modern farmland colonised the open, ice-scoured terrain and gradually created shallow soils. Cold-adapted trees, such as birch and pine, were able to take root and eventually vast areas of Britain came to be covered by dense forests.

At this time Britain was part of the Continent and the present-day English Channel was dry land. As the climate improved, more and more tree species were able to spread north. The colonisation stopped only when the rising sea level turned Britain into an island, but by this time two species of oak had reached Britain. Superbly adapted for the mild yet seasonal British climate, they came to dominate the forests, covering huge areas.

In the wetter and more mountainous north and west, the sessile or durmast oak *Quercus petraea* flourished. In the lowlands of the south and east, the pedunculate, common or English oak *Quercus robur* was prevalent. These two species are easily distinguished by their acorns. Those of the sessile oak sit in cups that have no stalks and grow directly from the twig – this is the meaning of the word 'sessile'. Pedunculate oak acorns grow on long stalks called peduncles, sometimes in small clusters.

Centuries of life

An oak can live for nearly a thousand years. The 300 years that it takes to reach full size may be followed by a further 300 years during which the oak gradually thickens its canopy, without dramatically changing its shape. It may then survive for another 300 years, undergoing a slow decline until, wizened and hollowed by age and decay, the tree finally succumbs to the attacks of fungi and dies.

Even after its death the oak has not reached the end of its usefulness, for the decaying trunk will be home to insect larvae, such as the grubs of the stag beetle. Fungi speed up the process of decay, until eventually the tree disappears back into the soil in the form of plant foods that will nourish other oak trees.

Throughout its very long life the oak will produce immense numbers of seeds. Every year, starting as a very young tree and continuing for centuries, each oak will provide a crop of

Forest oaks are the focus of life around them, the varying shade cast by their spreading crowns determining the pattern of shrub and herb growth below. Here, bluebells and wood spurge flower in the sunlight filtering through the newly emerged oak foliage of late spring.

TYPES OF OAK

Two species of oak are native to the British Isles, which means that they found their own way here and were not introduced by man. The pedunculate oak and the sessile oak share the same general features, but there are differences in form, structure and habitat preference that make them quite distinctive.

● **Sessile or durmast oak** (*Quercus petraea*) has broad yellowish green leaves which are lobed and have yellow stalks up to 1cm (½in) long. It is generally faster-growing than the pedunculate oak, with straighter branches and a longer trunk. It is found on the more acid soils of upland Britain, though if planted, this oak will grow quite happily in lowland areas. It is more resistant to wet climates than the pedunculate oak.

Pedunculate oak

The oak is a deciduous tree, losing all its leaves at the end of autumn.

The leaves of the sessile oak have relatively shallow lobes and each leaf grows on a short stalk.

Tree shape is determined by the openness of the location and prevailing weather pattern. Deer often browse the lower branches, producing a flat base to the tree.

An oak growing in the open will increase its circumference by about an inch each year. So measuring the girth of a tree in inches – at about 1.5m (5ft) above the ground – will give an estimate of its age: a girth of 250 inches means the tree is about 250 years old. If you measure in centimetres, divide by 2.5.

The pedunculate oak's leaves are similar in shape to those of the sessile oak, but they have much deeper lobes and almost no stalks.

● **Pedunculate, common or English oak** (*Quercus robur*) has longer, more deeply lobed leaves than the sessile oak, and they have virtually no stalks. The base of each leaf is often curled in around the midrib. The tree itself may be more broadly spreading with tangled branches. This species is more common in lowland areas and in the south and east of Britain, with many fine specimens growing in parklands. It is rare in north-west Scotland, and only scattered in western Ireland.

OAK GALLS

The large, spongy oak apple gall is caused by a gall wasp. It is pink or cream at first, but turns brown with age. Adult wasps emerge from the gall in the summer.

Spangle galls are very common on the underside of oak leaves. Each spangle contains the larva of a tiny gall wasp, which feeds on the nutritious gall tissue.

Sessile oaks are so called because their acorns grow directly on the twigs, without any obvious stalks. They generally grow singly or in pairs.

The common oak's acorns are described as pedunculate because they grow on long stalks or peduncles, sometimes in clusters as seen here.

● **Alien oaks**
The Turkey oak, holm oak and red oak have been introduced to the British Isles from Europe and Asia in the past few hundred years, and are now widespread.

tens of thousands of acorns. The ripening acorns fall in late autumn, and many are taken by woodland birds and mammals as food. Others will be infected with the burrowing larvae of weevils or die of fungus attack, but just a few will fall onto suitable patches of woodland floor and germinate to form tiny oak seedlings. Of these, only a small fraction will avoid the attentions of nibbling deer or rabbits to reach maturity, but

as long as just one seedling survives, there will be a tree to replace the parent oak when it finally dies.

Spring flowers

In a mature wood, many shrubs and trees grow among the oaks in places where light penetrates the leaf canopy, especially in pedunculate oak woodland on rich soils. In the spring, the ground beneath the oaks is a carpet of wild flowers and herbs, competing

for the light before the leaves in the oak canopy thicken up and block it out. Primroses, wood anemones, bluebells and early purple orchids grow among ferns, sedges and mosses, all taking advantage of the spring sunshine filtering through the virtually bare branches.

Meanwhile the buds of the oaks swell and burst open, and the trees begin to look green again after the dormant period of winter. The oak

flowers emerge first, before the leaves are fully open. They look like golden-green catkins, and release clouds of pollen that are carried from tree to tree by the wind.

The flowers may be eaten by dormice, hungry for a protein-rich source of food after their long hibernation, and the freshly opened leaves are often stripped back to the leaf stalks by millions of caterpillars. Fortunately, this seems to do little harm to the

◄ The many insects found around oaks are a rich food source for night-hunting pipistrelle bats, which catch their prey on the wing. The long-eared bat does the same, but can also pluck insects directly from the leaves.

▼ Jays are probably vital to the regeneration of the oak wood because new trees grow from acorns that the jays bury for use as winter food supplies.

The oak provides food for the great spotted woodpecker, which uses its powerful bill to hack into dead wood and loose bark in search of wood-boring insect larvae. The woodpecker also uses dead branches as resonant drumming posts in spring to attract a mate, and excavates its nesting holes in the timber.

trees, which quickly grow a second set of leaves. Since the main caterpillar season has then passed, most of these leaves survive for the rest of the summer.

▲ Migrant pied flycatchers, such as this female, breed when the caterpillar population on sessile oaks reaches its spring peak, providing plenty of food for their hungry brood of young.

Dawn chorus

Spring caterpillars are a vital food supply for breeding birds such as the blue tit and great tit, which time their nesting season to coincide with the caterpillar glut. The adult birds are kept very busy carrying food to their nestlings and the oak wood is full of activity, especially when the young are taking their first flights. The wood is also filled with birdsong, particularly at the beginning of the breeding season when the males are claiming their breeding territories. The dawn chorus, which actually starts before sunrise, can be a very noisy time because every songbird in the wood competes to be heard.

By late July or August the oak produces new shoots and leaves – often red – known as the 'Lammas Growth' after the church festival of Lammastide. But although this adds colour

to the canopy, the dense foliage of summer cuts out much of the light and the woodland floor becomes shadier and less colourful. The spring flowers have long vanished and the ground cover is a near-uniform green.

Yet throughout the wood, life continues at a busy pace. A huge variety of insects and spiders feed among the leaves, providing food for birds. Purple hairstreak butterflies flutter around the topmost branches by day while moths rest on the tree trunks, relying on their superb camouflage for protection. Moths become active at night, when most of the birds are roosting, but many fall victim to woodland bats, such as the long-eared bat, which locate their prey in the darkness by echo-location. The huge ears of the long-eared bat give it such fine discrimination that it can target insects sitting on leaves as well as those that are flying. Its broad, high-lift wings

enable it to fly very slowly and even hover among foliage, to pinpoint and then catch its victim.

Oak galls

Some insects have a curious effect on oak trees, making them sprout strange growths known as oak galls. The insects lay their eggs in the tree's buds, and the larvae that emerge from the eggs stimulate the tree into producing the galls, which feed and protect the larvae as they develop. Eventually, each larva turns into an adult insect that cuts a tiny hole in the gall, crawls out and flies away, leaving the empty gall on the tree.

The most familiar oak gall is the oak apple, a fleshy, fruit-like structure that is at its ripest in late May or June. It is home to many tiny wasp larvae and some of these will themselves contain even smaller parasitic larvae feeding on their tissues. The new

▲ The grey squirrel relies heavily on stored acorns for its survival through the winter months, but it switches to feeding on oak buds and flowers when they appear in spring.

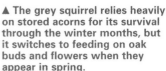

◄ In the undisturbed quiet of the oak wood, animal and insect life prospers.

▶ The spotted coat of a very young roe deer provides perfect camouflage on the sun-dappled forest floor of early spring. When it is not being fed by its mother, the kid instinctively remains motionless, usually lying down, and is almost impossible to see among the spring flowers.

▲ The badger's presence is betrayed by trails through the vegetation, occasional footprints, and fresh earth and discarded bedding at the entrance to its sett.

▲The silver-washed fritillary can sometimes be seen feeding on the nectar of brambles and thistles in sunny clearings. It lays its eggs on the trunks of oak trees, where the larvae hibernate before crawling down to feed on violets growing on the woodland floor.

► Oak trees come into full leaf relatively late in spring, allowing plenty of sunlight through the canopy. This provides woodland flowers, such as the wood anemone, with the energy they need to bloom and set seed.

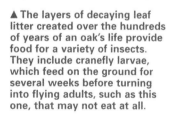

Where can I see oak woodlands?

Much of Britain's once extensive ancient oak forest has been cleared over the centuries to create farmland, but fragments remain including:

Wistman's Wood (Devon)
Yarner Wood (Devon)
The Menns (Sussex)
Borrowdale Woods (Cumbria)
Charnwood Forest (Leics.)
Devil's Bridge (Aberystwyth)
Eccleshall Woods (Sheffield)

You can see very old oak trees in:
Windsor Great Park (Berkshire)
Hatfield Forest (Essex)
Savernake Forest (Wiltshire)
Sherwood Forest (Notts)
New Forest (Hampshire)

For more information contact:
The Woodland Trust
The Forestry Commission
Local wildlife trusts

▲ The layers of decaying leaf litter created over the hundreds of years of an oak's life provide food for a variety of insects. They include cranefly larvae, which feed on the ground for several weeks before turning into flying adults, such as this one, that may not eat at all.

adults usually emerge from the gall in midsummer and fly off to lay their eggs on a different part of the tree.

Marble galls are more woody and each contains a single larva. Sometimes a nuthatch or great tit will peck into the gall to eat the larva, but otherwise the larva turns into a tiny wasp that emerges through a neat round hole in the gall. In recent decades the curious knopper gall has also become very common. This appears as a misshapen acorn that fails to germinate. The tiny insect that causes it spends part of its life in the

► The orange-tip butterfly flies from April to June, sipping nectar from spring flowers. The female lays her eggs on the buds of lady's smock. She does not have the male's orange wing patch, but does have the same mossy green pattern on her hind underwings.

peduncular oak and part in the Turkey oak, a species introduced from Asia.

Leaf litter
As the days shorten, the oaks begin to lose their leaves. They will be little use in winter, when light levels are low. If the season is really cold, rainwater turns to snow and ice, and the trees can suffer from a form of drought. Since oak leaves lose vast amounts of water to the air, the trees are better off without them. But first they recycle the useful materials in the leaves, and this is what makes

Named for the massive antler-like jaws of the male, the stag beetle can be seen for only a few weeks in early summer, when the adults fly in search of mates. Females lay eggs in rotting wood, which the larvae then eat.

◄ Dryad's saddle fungus grows on the rotting stumps of oaks and is responsible for the final stages of decay before the tree eventually disappears back into the soil. The brackets can be up to 50cm (20in) wide.

◄ Growing among the mosses and ferns on the shadiest of woodland floors, wood sorrel can be recognised by its clover-like leaves, which are fresh green above and purplish below.

► White admiral butterflies can often be seen along the overgrown verges of woodland rides and on the edges of clearings, where they feed on bramble nectar and breed on honeysuckle.

them change colour to yellow and then brown before they fall to the ground.

The cascades of dead leaves and other debris, such as bird droppings and dead insects, enrich the soil beneath the trees and provides food for fungi. These grow unseen for most of the year until the damp autumn weather encourages their fruiting bodies to appear above the ground as mushrooms and toadstools. The many types of fungi growing among the fallen leaves help break them down into plant nutrients, which then become available to the trees again.

Planting service

As summer turns to autumn, the ripening acorns attract hungry birds and mammals. Pigs forage beneath oaks growing in the New Forest, eating huge quantities in years of plenty. Acorns are also highly prized by grey squirrels and jays, which collect and store them away for the winter.

Squirrels bury the acorns in ones and twos over large areas of woodland, usually nibbling them a little first to prevent the acorns germinating and growing into new trees. Throughout the winter the squirrels forage over the woodland floor searching for their stored acorns and feeding on any that have not already been found by mice or other animals.

Unlike squirrels, jays bury acorns singly and unharmed, so they are more likely to grow

LIFE CYCLE OF AN OAK

FIRST YEAR
Through the spring, seedlings from acorns push up through the leaf litter. Those that survive woodland animals feeding on them grow quickly through the springtime and into summer.

GROWTH
The growing tree pushes its way through the shrub layer and into the lower canopy of the woodland. It keeps growing for many centuries, gradually spreading upward and outward.

MATURITY
Oaks reach maturity after about 300 years. They will not grow much more, but can remain in good, healthy condition for a further 300 years.

OLD AGE
The decline of an oak tree can take another 300 years, and the trunk is often hollowed out by fungi.

if they are not retrieved and eaten. Many of the fine oaks growing in our forests will have been planted by jays, the oak tree relying heavily on them to distribute its seeds. It has even been suggested that the acorn evolved especially to attract these birds.

Winter dormancy

After leaf fall in late autumn the true shape of the oak is revealed. Its strong trunk and rugged branches make it stand out against the more delicate hazels with which it often grows. At this time the oak is dormant, yet even in the very coldest weather there will still be life around the tree. The deep furrows in its bark and the scales on its leaf buds are

home to numerous tiny invertebrates, so the oak provides plenty of food for resident woodland birds such as treecreepers, nuthatches, goldcrests, wrens and tits. Hollows in very old trees are used as shelters by grey squirrels and owls, and cavities among the roots make weatherproof refuges for wood mice and voles.

At this time of year the oak wood seems a still, quiet place, but there is still plenty of activity, with occasional animal cries shattering the silence. On winter evenings the eerie screech of the fox carries over great distances and the barking alarm call of the otherwise quiet roe deer can

be startlingly loud. You may hear a badger snuffling through the undergrowth, or the rustle of a weasel hunting through the fallen leaves.

Throughout the year the oak trees have grown a little, each adding another growth ring to its trunk. Their buds form early, so when spring finally arrives again they are ready to burst into flower and spread their new leaves in the sun.

Glorious bluebell groves

Carpets of these wild flowers in full bloom are a stunning sight, but the mesmerising haze of blue is just the most dramatic feature of a rich wildlife habitat that supports a whole community of plants and animals.

Bluebells are seen at their purest blue on cloudy days, because bright sunlight gives them a purple tinge. As the flowers age, they fade to greyish blue.

The brimstone is one of the earliest butterflies in bluebell woods. Only males are the distinctive sulphur yellow; the females are greenish white.

Spring in the British countryside reaches its floral climax with the appearance of shimmering drifts of bluebells. This enchanting phenomenon is one of the highlights of the natural history calendar. It is a sight envied by plant lovers and botanists around the world, for only in Britain's mild and moist climate do bluebells grow with such vigour.

Wild hyacinth

Bluebells are basically wild hyacinths, closely related to the cultivated varieties that many people grow in containers. Indeed, the plant is sometimes known as wild hyacinth in Scotland, where the bluebell name refers instead to the summer flowering harebell of England. There are a variety of old country names as well, including culverkeys, auld man's bells, ring o' bells and jacinth. However, in most places 'bluebell' is the accepted name for the plant.

If it were not such a mouthful, it might be safer to refer to the bluebell by its precise scientific name of *Hyacinthoides non-scripta*. This name is derived from Greek mythology, in which the

The sight of a forest floor carpeted with bluebells is a sure sign that the soil has remained undisturbed for hundreds of years. Paradoxically, it is in woodland that is coppiced or sympathetically managed that the best displays are found.

Spartan prince Hyacinthus was accidentally killed by the god Apollo. The legend has it that hyacinths sprang up where his blood was shed and Apollo inscribed the letters AIAI – meaning 'alas' – on the flower as a mark of his remorse. As the bluebell, our native hyacinth, has no trace of these letters, it was named '*non-scripta*' – or 'unlettered'.

Ancient woodlands

Bluebells are known as 'oceanic' or 'Atlantic' plants because they are found mainly in western Europe where the climate is dominated by the influence of the Atlantic Ocean. Widely distributed throughout the British Isles, especially in the lowlands, they grow in a variety of habitats, including woods, hedgerows and grassland. Some lone specimens are even found clinging to treeless cliff ledges and ravines battered by fierce winds and sea spray. But although you may come across bluebells growing in such odd places, by far the greatest numbers occur in broad-leaved woodland that is dominated by giant oak trees.

This is because bluebells have a life cycle that is adapted to the rhythm of the seasons in deciduous woodland, where the trees drop their leaves in winter. In eastern counties in particular, they are most characteristic of ancient woodlands with a long history of continuous tree cover dating from before the 16th century. Such woodlands are much richer in wildlife than those more recently established and they can often be recognised by the presence of 'indicator plants', such as wood anemone and dog's mercury, which rarely grow in younger woods. Bluebells are less dependable indicators of the age of woodland habitats. In the Midlands they are sometimes found in younger woodlands, and on the west coast they are not confined to woods at all.

Their confusing distribution is a consequence of the fact that bluebells prefer moist habitats. Without forest cover during the summer, the soil dries out and bluebells cannot thrive. In wetter parts of the country, bluebells can survive without the protection of the tree canopy.

Spring bloom

Bluebells are adapted for life in oak woodland because they complete most of their life

---

PROTECTED!

The bluebell is afforded some protection by the 1981 Wildlife and Countryside Act, which states that it is an offence to uproot any wild plant without the landowner's permission. Plans have been instigated by the Joint Nature Conservation Committee to offer further legal protection, targeting the trade in bluebell bulbs, so conserving the woodland heritage for future generations to enjoy.

BLUEBELL FACT FILE

Bluebells grow best in open woodland, but are intolerant of waterlogging, drought, trampling and grazing. They are fairly resistant to frost damage, but continuous heavy shade severely reduces the production of leaves, flowers and seeds. Several disease-causing powdery moulds attack flowers and stems, causing bulb rot in wet soils. Insects, especially bumblebees, honeybees, butterflies and hover flies, are important pollinators of bluebells.

● **NAMES**
Common name: bluebell
Scientific name: *Hyacinthoides non-scripta*

● **HABITAT**
Oak, beech and ash woodland, hazel and chestnut coppice, hedgerows, rough grassland especially under recently felled woodland, cliff and rock ledges, dense scrub; tolerates a wide range of soil types, but prefers mildly acidic, moist soils

● **DISTRIBUTION**
Widely distributed throughout the British Isles, less common in Ireland, absent from Orkney and Shetland; most abundant below 340m (1120ft)

● **SIZE**
Height up to 50cm (20in); individual flowers up to 15–20mm (⅜–¾in) long

● **FLOWERS**
Up to 16 blue, insect-pollinated flowers per stalk; production of blue-violet, albino white or pink flowers may commence in the plant's fifth year

● **SEEDS**
Up to 100 rounded, charcoal black seeds, 2mm (⅟₁₆in) in diameter, per plant, housed in 15mm (⅝in) wide capsules suspended on slender stalks up to 50cm (20in) above the woodland floor; seeds germinate in low autumn temperatures

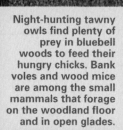

Solitary, early flowering bluebell plants look rather lost. It is not until the full mass of flowers appears that the species can be appreciated fully.

Night-hunting tawny owls find plenty of prey in bluebell woods to feed their hungry chicks. Bank voles and wood mice are among the small mammals that forage on the woodland floor and in open glades.

cycle early in the year, before the ground is shaded by the growing leaves in the tree canopy far overhead. It is truly a race against time, because once the canopy is complete very little light reaches the woodland floor. So the

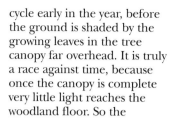

◄ In early spring, lesser celandines and common dog violets are among the first flowers to brighten up rides and clearings in bluebell woods. These two species are generally overwhelmed when the bluebells eventually form their dense stands.

▼ Morel fungi are spring specialists, with solitary specimens appearing beneath broad-leaved trees between March and May, especially in south-east England. The cap is riddled with honeycomb-like pits, and both the cap and stem are hollow.

bluebells grow, flower and set seed all in the space of a few critical weeks.

They are not alone. Lesser celandines and delicate wood anemones also grow and flower early in the season before the trees come into leaf and shade them out. Together with the bluebells, which bloom slightly later, they form a major part of the 'field layer' that carpets the woodland floor. During the rest of the year, the plants survive by adopting a kind of siege economy, locking away food in storage bulbs and tubers hidden deep in the soil until the following spring.

Thinning the canopy

Although bluebells are well equipped for survival in natural oak woodlands, they are at their most abundant in woods that have been managed for timber by the traditional technique of coppicing. This involves thinning out the great oaks, which opens up the canopy and allows more light to reach the ground, and cutting the other trees – usually hazel or chestnut – to ground level so that they sprout many slender shoots of young growth. The shoots of these coppiced trees are harvested after seven years and used for making fences, charcoal and other woodland products, and the oak is – or

DID YOU KNOW?

● Bluebells are the symbol for the Botanical Society of the British Isles.

● If you get thirsty after a rambling walk in a bluebell wood, the best place to be is in the East Midlands, where there are more pubs called 'The Bluebell' or 'The Blue Bell' than anywhere else in Britain!

● The 'Bluebell Railway' in East Sussex is so named because it passes through wooded countryside thronged with bluebells.

alongside the bluebells in recently cut clearings, and even when the coppice grows back. They create a mass of colour and scent, which is one reason why such woodland supports more butterfly species than any other habitat. Coppicing also encourages small mammals including shrews, bank voles, dormice and yellow-necked mice.

Traditional practices such as coppicing are rarely financially viable today, although there has been a recent revival of the technique as a tool for nature conservation. The sight of a bluebell wood in full bloom is a rich reward for the effort and expense involved.

Many layers

The field layer of bluebells and other flowers is just one of several layers in the woodland. Each layer is dominated by a particular type and stature of plant, and each supports a characteristic, yet diverse wildlife community.

Overhead, mature trees such as ash, beech and particularly oak dominate the tree canopy layer. This is where breeding birds feast on a plentiful springtime supply of insects, such as butterfly and moth caterpillars, leafhoppers,

sawflies, beetles and gall wasps feeding on and among the emerging leaves in the canopy. If you watch the foliage you will see warblers and tits busily hunting for leaf-eating and sap-sucking insects to eat

▶ The common bee-fly closely resembles and mimics the bumblebee, and thereby gains protection from predators. Common in early springtime in southern England, but rare elsewhere, it is often seen hovering and clinging to spring flowers, drinking their nectar.

Spanish bluebell escapees hybridise with native species and in some areas this is giving cause for concern that the newcomer may threaten the survival of the true British bluebell.

was – used for big building projects. This system provides a sustainable source of timber, and also creates a perfect habitat for bluebells and other woodland wildlife. The open, sunny coppiced woods are full of flowers in late spring. Wood anemone, wood spurge, primrose, early purple orchid and greater stitchwort flourish

A favourite with watercolour artists, bluebell woods can appear to shimmer as the dappled light catches the massed nodding flowers.

▲ Badgers have been known to uproot bluebell bulbs to supplement their diet in the bleak seasons of late autumn and winter, when their preferred foods – earthworms, grubs, small mammals and snails – can be hard to find.

▼ During the warmer months, whiskered bats emerge from their daytime roosts at dusk to hunt. They use echo-location to catch insects – a technique so efficient they can capture up to 10 moths a minute.

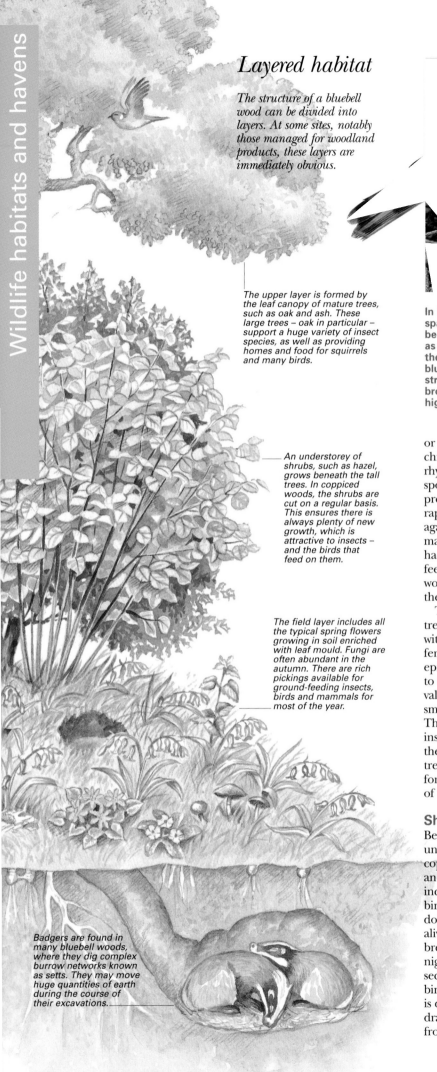

Layered habitat

The structure of a bluebell wood can be divided into layers. At some sites, notably those managed for woodland products, these layers are immediately obvious.

The upper layer is formed by the leaf canopy of mature trees, such as oak and ash. These large trees – oak in particular – support a huge variety of insect species, as well as providing homes and food for squirrels and many birds.

An understorey of shrubs, such as hazel, grows beneath the tall trees. In coppiced woods, the shrubs are cut on a regular basis. This ensures there is always plenty of new growth, which is attractive to insects – and the birds that feed on them.

The field layer includes all the typical spring flowers growing in soil enriched with leaf mould. Fungi are often abundant in the autumn. There are rich pickings available for ground-feeding insects, birds and mammals for most of the year.

Badgers are found in many bluebell woods, where they dig complex burrow networks known as setts. They may move huge quantities of earth during the course of their excavations.

In larger tracts of woodland, sparrowhawks can occasionally be seen hunting for prey such as small songbirds. In spring the female lays four to six bluish white eggs, usually strongly blotched with red-brown, in a substantial nest high in the tree canopy.

or carry back to their hungry chicks. You may hear the rhythmic drumming of a great spotted woodpecker as it proclaims its territory by rapidly hammering its bill against a dead branch – you may even see one. A slower hacking sound may be a feeding woodpecker digging wood-boring insects out of their tunnels in dead timber.

The gnarled bark of the trees is often thickly covered with ivy, lichens, mosses and ferns. Such plants are called epiphytes. They do little harm to the tree and provide valuable food and shelter for small woodland creatures. These plants attract other insect-hunting birds such as the nuthatch and mouse-like treecreeper, both specialists at foraging for prey on the bark of big trees.

Shrub and coppice

Below the canopy layer is an understorey dominated by coppiced hazel and chestnut, and young trees and shrubs including the field maple, birch, holly, hawthorn and dogwood. This shrub layer is alive with the noisy singing of breeding birds, not least the nightingale. Although this secretive, brown, russet-tailed bird is rarely seen, its presence is declared by the beautiful, dramatic song that emanates from thorny thickets and

young coppice. The elusive dormouse can also be found in the dense undergrowth of the shrub layer, where it often builds its nest from the shredded bark of honeysuckle.

Flowers and butterflies

Beneath the understorey lies the field layer, with its fragrant drifts of bluebells and other herbaceous plants. Stand very still and you may hear the quiet rustlings of a bank vole foraging among the spring flowers, or possibly a nocturnal wood mouse if you are out in a woodland clearing at dusk. The flowers also provide food for a variety of woodland butterflies including the white admiral, speckled wood and several species of fritillary.

Beneath the surface

Below the field layer is a ground cover of diminutive mosses and moist drifts of dead leaves shed in previous years. The colour and texture of this dead material is mimicked superbly by the highly camouflaged woodcock. This is the only British wader that lives in woodland, where it uses its long bill to probe the

A touch of yellow is provided by clumps of primroses, which appear along woodland rides and in sunny clearings among the bluebells themselves.

◀ The secretive woodcock is particularly well camouflaged as it crouches quietly on damp, dead leaves during the day, emerging at dusk to search for earthworms. The woodcock breeds throughout Britain. It lays a clutch of up to five eggs in April, in a simple nest made of fallen leaves on the woodland floor.

soft ground for worms, beetle grubs and other soil animals. If you turn over a dead log you will see the ground beneath come to life as the uncovered invertebrates scramble to escape the light.

Many of these invertebrates live on or in dead wood, as do fungi such as the curious morel. Along with armies of woodlice and millipedes, fungi play an important role in helping to break down the organic matter on the woodland floor, recycling nutrients back to the living organisms in the ecosystem.

Bluebells in danger

Bluebells used to be harvested for their bulbs. These are poisonous in their fresh state, but when dried and powdered they have been used in herbal medicines. The sticky mucilage in the bulbs was once used as a gum for bookbinding, and even as a starch substitute for stiffening Elizabethan ruffs.

In recent years bluebell bulbs have been illegally stripped from some woods to sell as garden flowers – although they never look the same in small numbers, and can become a problem by spreading in small gardens. They are best enjoyed in the wild, but even here they may be in danger.

If Britain's climate continues to warm up, there could be severe consequences for the bluebell and other springtime flowers. These plants are relatively insensitive to low winter temperatures and start growing early in the season, unlike invasive plants such as

► The chestnut-coloured bank vole is typical of dense woodland thickets and hedgerows where it forages for food during the day and night. Bluebell bulbs, flowers and seeds provide a tasty protein-rich addition to its usual diet of moss, leaves and fruit.

cow parsley which are spurred into growth later in spring by rising temperatures. If Britain starts to get warmer winters, then the bluebells could lose their competitive advantage. They might be overwhelmed by rival plants, and start to disappear. It seems almost inconceivable, but they could even be lost from our flora altogether.

Northumberland's nature trails

Great ice sheets grinding over hard volcanic rock created this county's dramatic landscapes. In spring their rugged grandeur is softened by a rich variety of colourful flowers and the evocative calls of breeding birds.

Northumberland is the most northerly county of England. Its northern edge lies along the border with Scotland, and its rugged, unyielding terrain forms wild, spectacular landscapes that are beloved of hill walkers. Yet despite its air of remote wilderness it is still relatively accessible to visitors, the whole area lying within easy reach of some of the north's largest cities. At its heart is Northumberland National Park, 1049 square kilometres (405 square miles) of upland, which was designated in 1955 in recognition of its wonderful scenery and its special merits as a wildlife haven.

The appearance of the landscape and the nature of its vegetation, owe much to the actions of fire and ice. Most of the region's geological backbone was formed by a combination of ancient volcanic processes, the sedimentary deposition of layers of limestone, sandstone and shale, and the subsequent intrusion of lava flows into these layers. The erosive power of ice during successive ice ages helped to create the surface topography, scouring the land and removing many layers of sediment.

The influence of people on the Northumbrian landscape is also striking. In particular, Hadrian's Wall – more correctly known as the Roman Wall and now a World Heritage Site – is one of the county's finest archaeological features. One of the best preserved stretches of the Wall passes along the southern border of the National Park.

Lonely landscapes

The journey from north to south through the National Park starts at the Scottish border and passes down the Cheviot Hills. A hike through this uncompromising country takes you through lonely, remote places, and many of the landmarks have evocative or strange-sounding names, such as Beefstand, Russell's Cairn, Bloodybush Edge, Cushat Law and Comb Hill. At Windy Gyle, the softly rounded lava flows from a long-extinct volcano form a ring around the Cheviot – which at 815m (2674ft) is Northumberland's highest hill. The walking is strenuous but not precipitous, and the scene is enlivened by most of the birds typically associated with moorland habitats.

South of the Cheviot Hills, and separated from them by the valley of the River Coquet, lies the impressive sandstone ridge known as the Simonside Hills. This area is at its best in August, when the pinkish purple flowers of ling (common heather) and rich magenta bell heather are in full and glorious bloom on the moorlands.

◀ Bell heather grows on the drier areas of heath. Elsewhere it is replaced by ling, or common heather, and by cross-leaved heath on wet ground.

◀ Hardy Swaledale sheep graze much of Northumberland's rough pasture. Grazing keeps scrub at bay and encourages low-growing herbs and grasses.

▲ Curlews breed on the high moors in spring. The females stay with their mottled chicks in scarcely concealed ground nests for five weeks.

The Roman Wall was begun in about AD 120, by order of Emperor Hadrian. At that time, the surrounding countryside would have harboured several wild animals that have since disappeared, including wild boar, beavers and wolves.

FLORAL SPECIALITIES

Subtle changes in the soil or rock chemistry often create small pockets of real botanical delights. For instance, where areas of damp grassland are influenced by standing pools of water rich in base minerals, such as calcium and magnesium, there is a chance of discovering such gems as ragged-robin, water avens, globeflower, melancholy thistle and grass-of-Parnassus. On lime-rich rock outcrops, you may come across colonies of starry and mossy saxifrage, roseroot, alpine saw-wort and alpine willowherb.

▶ Roseroot grows in tiny cracks in exposed rocks. The roots were once crushed to produce a rose-like scent.

▼ Alpine willowherb is a plant of mossy mountain streamsides, found on only a few isolated sites in northern England.

▶ Grass-of-Parnassus has heart-shaped leaves and pale cup-like flowers. It grows on moorland and damp upland pastures.

◄Wood warblers stand out from other warblers because their underparts have a bright yellow tinge. They arrive later and leave earlier in the summer than other migrant warblers.

▼ Patches of open woodland are ideal for redstarts such as this handsome male. This welcome summer visitor arrives in April and leaves by August.

West of the Simonsides is the Otterburn Training Area of the British Army. This covers roughly one fifth of the entire park and is out of bounds for most of the year since it is used as a practice firing range, often with live ammunition.

Heading south again, you reach the gently undulating valleys of the River Rede and then the North Tyne. Passing the eastern flanks of the Kielder Forest, you come to the Great Whin Sill in the south of the park. Formed when molten magma intruded between layers of sedimentary rock, this massive escarpment makes a natural fortification that formed a convenient base for much of Hadrian's Wall.

Oak woodlands

Long ago, much of the land that lies within the National Park was naturally forested with woodlands of hazel, ash, rowan and silver birch, dominated by the hardy sessile oak. These days, many of the remaining woods are probably best described as semi-natural, because they have been planted or altered by man. Yet they look wild enough, for their trees are festooned with lichens and mosses and they support a rich ground layer of wild plants, including bluebells, wood anemones and the scarcer chickweed wintergreen.

In spring and summer, resident woodland birds such as robins, song thrushes and

Northumberland's sessile oak woodlands are wild, magical places that echo to the chorus of breeding birds on spring mornings.

wrens are joined by migrant visitors including blackcaps, chiffchaffs and willow warblers, and mature open glades may harbour a migrant threesome that are often found together – redstart, pied flycatcher and wood warbler.

Although many patches of oak woodland survive, the predominant vegetation type these days is moorland. Such terrain can seem monotonous compared to the woods, but the moors vary in character according to a variety of geological and climatic factors, including the underlying rock type, the natural drainage and the elevation.

Grass and heather

The grasslands that are typical of many of the lower slopes of the Cheviots are grazed by flocks of hardy hill sheep, which keeps the grass short and prevents heather from growing. Their close cropping encourages plants such as heath bedstraw, tormentil and milkwort, all of which have small flowers that stud the short turf like jewels in spring and early summer.

As you climb the hills, grassland habitats often give way to heather moorland with

SHADY KIELDER FOREST

▲ The crossbill feeds on the seeds in conifer tree cones. It uses its crossed bill to prise the cone scales apart, then extracts the seeds with its tongue.

The largest of three separate forests that together form the Border Forest Park, the Kielder Forest is a plantation of exotic conifers, particularly spruces and pines. It was established on land that was formerly open moorland, and remains Europe's largest man-made forest.

Conifer plantations have a few saving graces in wildlife terms. The main benefit for native species is that in the early years after planting, these woodlands encourage a local population explosion of meadow pipits and small mammals, and they provide an ideal nesting habitat for predatory birds such as short-eared owls and merlins.

As they grow, conifer plantations contain relatively little in the way of wildlife,

because the dense canopy and the carpet of fallen needles prevents the growth of ground layer plants. Roe deer are nevertheless common here and are sometimes seen feeding in open rides and clearings. Red squirrels live unobtrusively in the trees, where they are occasionally preyed upon by the elusive pine marten.

Birds of the Kielder Forest include the crossbill, which relies on the seed-bearing cones of mature conifer trees for food. In recent years, goshawks have begun to nest in the mature conifer trees, where they prey on squirrels and birds.

▶ The magnificent goshawk is doing well in the protected depths of Kielder Forest. Once very rare, its recovery is aided by abundant prey and a decline in persecution by gamekeepers.

▲ The red squirrel has one of its few English strongholds in Kielder – the grey squirrel is for once at a disadvantage in purely coniferous forest.

▶ The nimble pine marten is one of the few mammal predators capable of catching a red squirrel. The English population almost became extinct in the early 20th century, but its fortunes have revived.

boggy mires. Bright green swathes of *Sphagnum* moss mark the wettest patches, and these boggy, acid locations also support plants such as cottongrass, harestail, heath spotted orchid, bog asphodel, cranberry and deergrass, as well as the insect-eating round-leaved sundew.

Towards the drier margins of the mires, bog myrtle begins to colonise and soon gives way to bell heather, ling, bilberry, crowberry and cowberry. There is even a chance of discovering the local and elusive dwarf cornel, chickweed wintergreen or

lesser twayblade orchid among the dominant stands of taller moorland plants.

Bracken has colonised many of the lower slopes in the park. Its dense growth can make the discovery of low-growing plants difficult, but a search in spring, before the fronds are too large, sometimes reveals pockets of unexpected plants such as bluebells, wood crane's-bill and woodruff.

Wood crane's-bill blooms in the hedgerows in late spring and early summer, and forms a mass of colour in the traditional hay meadows near Alwinton.

◄ Shovelers feed in shallow water, straining beakfuls of mud for tiny animals. These handsome ducks (this is a male) can be seen all year round in parts of the park.

► Good light reveals the subtle beauty of the male wigeon. Although most numerous in winter, a few wigeon remain in the region to breed in spring and summer while the rest fly further north.

Breeding birds

In spring, the highlight of a visit to the park's higher ground will be the breeding waders. On calm, dry mornings the air rings with the calls of curlews, golden plovers, lapwings, dunlins, redshanks and snipe. Several songbirds are to be found here too, with the ubiquitous meadow pipit nesting on the grassland and heather moors, and ring ouzels and wheatears favouring rocky outcrops.

Taking advantage of the abundant prey in the breeding season are merlins and peregrines, which feed mainly on smaller birds, and short-eared owls and kestrels, which hunt mainly for small mammals such as field voles.

Their presence is an indication that the area was once wooded. Several valley slopes are covered with gorse, a shrub that competes well with bracken. The sweetly almond-scented, golden-yellow flowers can be seen throughout the year, but are at their best from April to June.

◄ The big, shiny buttercup-like flowers of marsh-marigold bring the first splash of spring colour to the shallow margins of lakes in the National Park.

Anyone who has walked in this region will be familiar with the local red grouse, which take to the wing explosively in alarm, uttering their loud '*go-back, go-back, go-back*' calls. In some areas the heather moorland is systematically burned to create a mosaic of young heather shoots and tall cover for these valuable gamebirds. Their larger cousin, the black grouse, lives on the wild moors and is very elusive. In recent years its numbers have declined dramatically.

Kielder Water is a man-made reservoir that attracts many waterbirds. It is fringed with planted conifer forests that provide a refuge for red squirrels and goshawks.

The clear, fast-flowing Upper Coquet, which divides the Otterburn Training Area, is an important spawning river for salmon. Their spectacular upstream migration can be admired from many vantage points.

Places to visit in Northumberland

From Hadrian's Wall in the south to the Scottish border in the north, this is a region of dramatic hill country. Exploration of its grasslands and woodlands, as well as its fells, is rewarding at any time of the year, but in spring especially, the landscape is graced by a rich diversity of flowers and nesting birds.

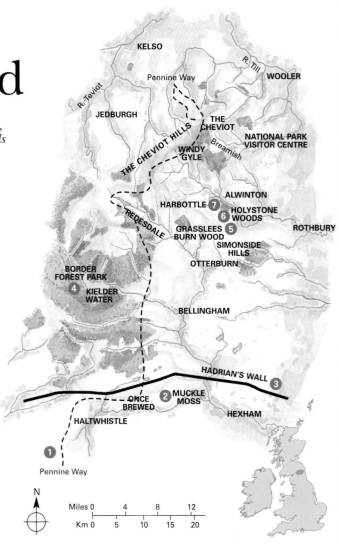

1 The Pennine Way
The Pennine Way is a long-distance route that winds its way through the whole length of Northumberland National Park, following Hadrian's Wall in the south and the Scottish border in the north. All the Northumbrian habitats can be seen along the length of the Pennine Way, and by following its course you will see much of the National Park's wildlife.

2 Muckle Moss
You need a permit to visit this unique valley bog system, which harbours rare wetland plants and dragonflies.

3 Hadrian's Wall
You may visit the Wall for its historic significance rather than its wildlife appeal, but certain stretches offer superb views over the surrounding countryside that can be good for watching birds of prey.

4 Border Forest Park
The Border Forest Park embraces open moorland as well as Kielder Water and Kielder Forest and two other conifer plantations. The moors are inhabited by a wide variety of moorland birds, plus a herd of feral goats. The conifer plantations provide a home for a small but select band of specialised creatures, including red squirrels and crossbills. Kielder Water is good for wildfowl in winter.

5 Grasslees Burn Wood
This nature reserve is managed jointly by the Northumberland Wildlife Trust and Northumberland County Council. It is located in the valley of the Grasslees Burn, which separates the Simonside and Harbottle Hills. The damp woodland is dominated by moisture-tolerant alder trees that support an interesting range of birds, including breeding pied flycatchers.

6 Holystone Woodlands
The Northumberland Wildlife Trust manages two woodlands at Holystone as nature reserves and public access is permitted along marked trails. Both woodlands are classed as semi-natural, having been either planted or influenced by man. Holystone North Wood comprises gnarled and stunted sessile oaks in a moorland setting. By contrast, Holystone Burn Wood consists mainly of birches and juniper, sheltered in a valley bottom.

7 Harbottle Crags
Some of the best examples of dry heather moorland and waterlogged bog can be found at the nature reserve at Harbottle Crags. This rich site is managed by Northumberland Wildlife Trust and Forest Enterprise. Glacial erratics – rocks transported by ice – an ancient millstone quarry and a full range of moorland birds and plants can be found here.

In spring, adders and common lizards can be found sunbathing among the heather. Conspicuous insects include emperor, northern eggar and fox moths, and the small heath butterfly.

Clear streams
Rivers and streams within the National Park are generally clear, fast-flowing and relatively unpolluted, so they support good populations of insects such as the larvae of caddis flies, mayflies and stoneflies. They are hunted by dippers, and the adult insects are taken by grey wagtails.

Salmon and trout grace some of the swifter waters. These attract the attention of the region's otters, which are now doing well after an absence of many decades.

Standing open water is at a premium in the park and many of the best sites are located close to Hadrian's Wall in the south. Loughs such as Greenlee, Grindon and Broomlee are fringed by mire vegetation, including meadowsweet, marsh-marigold and mare's-tail. Nearby Kielder Water, in the middle of Kielder Forest, is a big draw for birds, particularly wintering wildfowl, such as whooper swans, wigeons, shovelers and goosanders. Many are still to be seen in early spring, before they fly back north for the summer.

The handsome whooper swan is a winter visitor from the northern tundra, but the birds generally stay in the region until about April.

WILDLIFE WATCH

How can I find out more about Northumberland National Park?

● For further information, write to the Northumberland National Park at Eastburn, South Park, Hexham, Northumberland, NE46 1BS, call 01434 605555, or visit www.nnpa.org.uk

● The park has three visitor centres. Once Brewed is the largest, due to its proximity to Hadrian's Wall – call 01434 344396 for details.

The best centre for wildlife enthusiasts, however, is further north at Ingram; contact 01665 578248.

● For more details about when to visit and where to go to see wildlife, call the Northumberland Wildlife Trust on 0191 284 6884, or contact their visitor centre at Hawkesby Nature Reserve on 01665 711578.

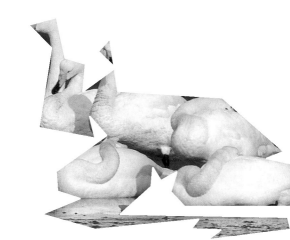

Animals and plants in focus

Grassland watch

- The rabbit
- The bank vole
- The barn owl
- Recognising buntings
- The dung beetle
- Wild grasses
- Golden dandelions

The rabbit

An unmistakable sight in fields, woods and on any open grassland, these alert and inquisitive creatures are often deemed a nuisance because of their destructive feeding habits, but remain one of Britain's most popular animals.

Although it is so familiar that it seems like a native animal, the rabbit was in fact introduced to Britain from France by the Normans about 900 years ago. Originally, it was a major economic asset – a rapidly reproducing and conveniently sized source of fur and food arriving at a time when storage of meat from larger animals presented major problems.

Rabbits were kept in special walled enclosures called warrens – a term used today for any rabbit colony and its burrows. They were looked after by a warrener who fed them and provided protection from predators and poachers. Sometimes, rabbits had access to surrounding fields farmed by local peasants but returned to the warren for shelter.

Escapes were inevitable and rabbits became established on sandy heaths and clifftops where the soil was easy to dig and too poor for farming. As a result, nobody bothered to exterminate the escaped rabbits and their numbers steadily increased, especially in the south of England.

Population explosion

In the 1700s, a major change in farming practice hugely benefited the rabbit. All over England, especially in the Midlands, extensive hedgerows were created to enclose farmland. These provided rabbits with shelter from the weather and cover from predators, right alongside huge fields of food. They emerged from their burrows to fan out and devastate crops. Even today, corn planted near hedgerows is often eaten in spring, exposing bare soil, while further out it is nibbled short, and appears a different colour from the main part of the field, away from the safety of the hedgerow.

Feral rabbits were often encouraged by the gentry, who valued them for hunting. At the same time, throughout the late 18th, 19th and early 20th centuries, rabbits benefited from landowners' and gamekeepers' ruthless persecution of predators that threatened other game, such as pheasants and grouse.

However, as a result of the damage they caused, most people considered rabbits to be a nuisance that could be harvested as part of the rural economy. So rabbits were trapped, snared and shot for their skins and meat. Millions were killed annually, yet there seemed to be no decline in their numbers. Shooting rabbits became a

Young rabbits come out to bask in the sunshine at the burrow entrance when they are about three weeks old. There may be up to seven or more in a litter. Inexperienced juveniles are very vulnerable to predators.

▲ Rabbits need to be constantly on the lookout for danger, since they are vulnerable to many predators. In long grass their view is obscured, so they often sit upright to check their surroundings. In short turf, they do not need to sit up so often.

RABBIT FACT FILE

Vulnerable to many predators, the rabbit's defences include acute hearing, keen eyesight, quick reactions and the ability to change direction at speed. They are well camouflaged – the sight of their flashing white tails as they head for their burrows at the first sign of danger is often the only indication of their presence.

● **NAMES**
Common name: rabbit
Scientific name: *Oryctolagus cuniculus*

● **HABITAT**
Field edges, grasslands, farmland, open deciduous woodland, heathland, road verges and railway embankments, large gardens and allotments, sand dunes; not normally found in wet places or on high moorland

● **DISTRIBUTION**
Throughout Britain, including Ireland and most of the Scottish islands

● **STATUS**
Very abundant in places and regarded as a pest; population crashes frequent, with perhaps 70% or more dying in a short time. Most recent population estimates are in the region of 38 million individuals at start of breeding season

● **SIZE**
Head and body length up to 400mm (16in); tail about 30mm (1¼in); adult body weight 1.2–2kg (2–4½lb); both sexes similar in size

● **KEY FEATURES**
Grey-brown body, greyish white belly and orange-buff on the neck; big ears, up to 70mm (3in) long; hind feet 75–95mm (3–4in) long; large brown eyes; tail black on top, fluffy white below

● **HABITS**
Normally lives in social groups, rarely far from cover or from burrow entrances; feeding and other activity mostly at night, but also often seen during the day

● **VOICE**
Various soft, throaty growls when angry or excited; loud, high-pitched screaming when caught by predators

● **FOOD**
Mainly grasses and cereal crops in summer, plus other crops and wild plants; leaves and young shoots of trees and tree bark, especially in winter

● **BREEDING**
Mainly from late January to late July, peaks April–May; litters of 3–7 or more young (average 5) produced at about 5 week intervals; 4–6 litters per year

● **NEST**
Usually uses burrows, often in groups, but may make a temporary nest on the surface

● **YOUNG**
Identified by smaller size and shorter ears

● **SIGNS**
Burrows average about 15cm (6in) in diameter; in places a little narrower or wider (up to about 40cm/16in); clusters of compact spherical droppings

Rabbits frequently groom their fine fur to prevent it from becoming matted and losing its vital insulating properties. Living underground, rabbits get dirt in their fur, which must be groomed out. After rain, the problem is worse because the burrow may well be muddy. This is why rabbits prefer to burrow into slopes or in well-drained soils.

Distribution map key

Present all year round

Not present

Sensitive ears can be turned independently in any direction, providing maximum information about the surroundings.

The twitching nose gives the impression that the rabbit is constantly sniffing for danger. In fact, it relies much more on its acute hearing and almost all-round vision to alert it to the presence of possible predators.

Rabbit fur is famously warm and soft, but it loses these qualities if it becomes wet. Rabbits are careful to avoid a soaking whenever possible.

Rabbit radar

While hopping along, the rabbit picks up a sound that might mean danger. Rather than continuing to run, perhaps straight into trouble, it stops to find out more about the situation.

Poised and motionless, the rabbit searches for signs of predators by rotating its ears through 360°. When it has located a possible source of danger, one ear keeps it under surveillance while the other checks for further hazards in the vicinity.

popular sport, with an obvious benefit for arable crops. Professional rabbit catchers earned a living keeping numbers down on farms and around villages.

Biological warfare

By the mid 20th century, rabbits had become Britain's most serious mammalian pest, doing more economic damage than rats and mice combined. Their depredations were estimated to cost over £50 million each year (equivalent to

more than £250 million today). In 1953, the myxoma virus was deliberately introduced to the rabbit population, and spread like wildfire. The virus was transmitted by rabbit fleas, and easily spread between individuals in confined burrows and underground nests. Blood-sucking mosquitoes carried it over wider distances.

The resulting disease, myxomatosis, was particularly nasty and almost always fatal. Within days, it caused swellings of the eyes and genital region. Soon the animal became blind. Unable to feed properly, an infected rabbit hopped around aimlessly, finally dying after about 11–15 days. In just two years, myxomatosis killed more than 99.99 per cent of the rabbit population. The devastation was so bad that numbers in some parts of Britain did not recover for 20 years.

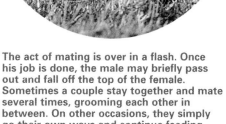

The act of mating is over in a flash. Once his job is done, the male may briefly pass out and fall off the top of the female. Sometimes a couple stay together and mate several times, grooming each other in between. On other occasions, they simply go their own ways and continue feeding.

In addition to highly sensitive ears, the rabbit has keen eyes, which it uses to scan its surroundings for any potential threat.

Turn tail and run!

The white flash of a rabbit's tail is very eye-catching. It acts as a warning to other rabbits, alerting them that some of their number are already running away from trouble.

▲ At birth, baby rabbits are blind and helpless. Their mother remains with them all day and only goes out at night to feed herself, carefully sealing the burrow entrance with soil behind her.

▶ By five days old, the babies – called kittens – already look more like adults. The first litters of the year normally start to appear above ground in early February, and the mothers then produce several more litters in the same year. This enables rabbit populations to build up rapidly.

But while crops and wild plants were relieved of the effects of rabbit damage, predators, such as buzzards, were deprived of an important source of food.

Today, myxomatosis is still present in the rabbit population, but the virus has weakened and rabbits seem to be less affected by it. Outbreaks now typically kill 40–60 per cent of infected animals, but rapid breeding easily makes up for such losses in a short time.

Recently, another fatal illness – rabbit haemorrhagic disease – has killed many animals, but it appears not to have swept the country with such devastating effects. Despite these setbacks, rabbit numbers are still high – annual crop damage is estimated to cost about £120 million or more nowadays.

Quick reactions are vital to a rabbit – being able to start, stop and change direction immediately may save it from becoming a meal. The rabbit's short front legs cause the white undertail or 'scut' to flash as it bobs along.

Family life

The rabbit is an exceptionally prolific animal. It starts to breed as early as January and may continue until August or even later. Females can produce up to seven or more young every five weeks or so throughout the summer. However, in high-density populations, breeding success is lower. Bad weather also reduces the rate of reproduction. Nevertheless, a single female may produce 20–30 offspring in a year – and these babies can breed at four months old, increasing the year's total substantially. Small wonder that by late summer some areas may have as many as 40 or more rabbits per hectare (2½ acres).

Courtship involves much dashing about, with the male leaping past the female, often urinating on her at the same time. Mating is a very rapid process, taking only a few seconds. It takes place frequently and actually stimulates the female to ovulate, so rabbit sex results in conception more frequently than that of some other animals. When she is ready to give birth, a pregnant rabbit normally digs a short burrow, 1–2m (3–6½ft) long. This is called a 'stop' and has only one entrance and no side branches. Alternatively, she may use a blind tunnel off one of the main burrows in a warren or, rarely, nest above ground. At the end of the stop, the mother-to-be makes a special nursery nest out of grass, moss or other plant material, and lines it with fur plucked from her own chest.

Female rabbit fur is normally well anchored to the skin, but the hormonal changes associated with pregnancy ensure that the fur of her chest and belly becomes looser and is easily pulled from the skin without discomfort. This fluffy bed will receive the young as they are born, and the mother crouches over her babies to suckle them. When she has to go to the surface, she carefully seals the entrance of the burrow behind her to reduce the risk of predators finding her young. Many mother rabbits return only once each night to feed their offspring.

The young are pink and blind when they are born, covered in a faint wispy fur. Their eyes open at about 10 days and they begin to appear at the entrance to the stop at about three weeks of age. They are weaned, that is they can feed themselves, at about 25 days old, and may disperse. Those born later in the season may remain with their mother for much longer. During normal activity, rabbits rarely go more than 100m (about 300ft) from the safety of their burrow, but when they first become independent, young males may disperse up to 800m (½ mile) or more from where they were born. Females disperse less frequently and usually over smaller distances.

Warrens and territories

The rabbit is a social species, living in small groups in a cluster of burrows. The dominant males rule the home and father most of the offspring. Females may fight fiercely to establish dominance among themselves, the winners gaining access to the best breeding sites. Adult females frequently attack their younger sisters, while the males may sometimes defend the youngsters. Subordinate females are usually the youngest of the adults, born the same year and breeding for the first time. They will often have a shorter breeding season and be forced to make their stops away from the main burrow system. Here their babies are more vulnerable to predators such as foxes and badgers. The offspring of dominant females are more likely to become dominant themselves and command the best nest sites near the centre of the warren.

Each social group of rabbits sets up a group territory by running up and down the boundaries in full view of their neighbours to establish which group lives where. They define the territory with scent from their paws, creating shallow scrapes in the soil and leaving the scent as

Living alongside crop fields provides rabbits with a constant food supply in spring and summer – the perimeters are often nibbled back to bare earth.

The rabbit's eyes are very sensitive to movement and also highly effective in poor light conditions at night. However, they are unable to distinguish between different colours to any great extent.

a marker. These scrapes are most numerous where rabbit territories meet. Strongly scented droppings are often deposited in clusters at the edge of the scrape or on top of a nearby ant mound or other prominent feature. Then the rabbits urinate on them, so the whole latrine is unmistakable.

Survival rate

Large rabbit populations consume a lot of food and as autumn progresses and plant growth slows, many rabbits die from shortages. Over winter, population densities are usually between one and 15 per hectare (2½ acres), depending on food availability. Highest numbers seem to be reached in areas of light sandy soils.

Although many babies are born in the spring and summer, the survival rate is low. The average life expectancy of a newborn rabbit is about 11 weeks, and at least three-quarters usually die within the year. Sometimes up to 95 per cent of young animals will not survive to breed the following year.

There is also a marked difference in survival rates between young males and females. Males have to live a much more dangerous life than females, going off to find new territory or, if they remain in the warren, patrolling the outer limits of existing territory, far from the safety of the burrows. Their lifestyle makes them vulnerable to attack by predators and as a result there are usually three females to every two males in the adult population.

Young rabbits are the preferred food of many predators, from buzzards to stoats and foxes or farm and feral cats, as well as weasels and badgers. Owls, great

black-backed gulls and other birds will take rabbits, and many other species eat them as carrion. Road traffic kills many, especially at night when they are dazzled by headlights. Despite this, often more than half of the mature adults survive from one year to the next.

Rabbit food

Rabbits like to live and feed in areas of short grass, close to their burrows – in fact they maintain this type of habitat by their feeding. They rarely go far into long grass, partly because they do not like to eat coarse vegetation and partly because tall grass tends to be wet from rain or dew, causing the rabbit's fur to become soggy and matted. Also, in long vegetation they cannot see approaching predators, so they stay out in the open. Rabbits are particularly successful in lowland areas with well-drained soil, such as sand dunes and chalk downland. The soft fescue grasses that grow in these areas are a favourite food, and the terrain means their burrows remain dry, even in winter.

Apart from soft grasses, preferred food includes horseshoe vetch, clover and crops. They will also gnaw the bark of trees, especially if snow covers their normal food supplies. At this time, much damage can be done to young trees and shrubs. At other times, the rabbits nibble shoots and leaves on tiny saplings, preventing growth of woody vegetation. Much of this material is indigestible because mammals do not possess the necessary digestive juices to break down cellulose, the principal component of plant cell walls. However, many bacteria and other micro-organisms can do so and cultures of these organisms thrive in a section of the rabbit's gut. They digest the cellulose, releasing nutritious contents.

Consequently, the rabbit's droppings often contain 15 per cent protein and much else that has escaped digestion. These first droppings are soft, black and moist, coated with a slimy mucus – and rabbits habitually eat them immediately, passing the food through their digestive system a second time. This process is called 'refection', and by doing this the rabbits reclaim much of what would otherwise be wasted. The droppings second time round are the familiar firm and dry, spherical 'rabbit currants'.

Where can I see rabbits in the wild?

● Rabbits pop up all over the place, but are often seen basking in the evening sunshine along hedges and field margins.

● Railway embankments are frequently colonised by rabbits and it's worth watching for them from passing trains.

● In parks and gardens, rabbits may become quite tame and approachable, but they are usually controlled because of the damage they do to plants.

Relaxed but ever-watchful

Rabbits spend a lot of time curled up underground or hunched up feeding, and this can cause muscle fatigue and poor circulation.

Just like tired humans, rabbits often stop what they are doing and stretch. But even though they may look relaxed, their ears are still busy scanning for the sound of predators.

Rabbits often yawn when they are tired, exposing their 'buck' teeth.

The bank vole

An industrious inhabitant of hedgerows, woodlands and scrub, the elusive and fast-moving bank vole is far more common than most people realise.

The countryside is filled with a multitude of small mammals that normally remain hidden from sight in the undergrowth. Among the most ubiquitous is the bank vole – a creature found almost everywhere in bushy and woodland habitats. It thrives in hedgerows, woodlands and even in rural and suburban gardens. Standing by a patch of brambles, you could have at least five bank voles within a few paces in any direction.

There are literally millions of these tiny mammals in the British Isles, but unlike the field vole, they rarely stray into the open because they are attractive and easy prey for predatory birds, foxes and other carnivorous mammals. Finding itself in the open, a bank vole will head for cover as quickly as it can, scurrying very fast and looking rather like a sausage, apparently propelled without legs. This is in contrast to the wood mouse, another common species of the countryside, which bounds like a tiny kangaroo and appears distinctly pale, with a long tail and legs.

All voles have short tails and legs, which are hidden by the body, a blunt, snub nose, tiny, inconspicuous ears and relatively small eyes. As well as these basic vole features, bank voles have a glossy, reddish brown back, creamy buff or grey belly and a two-tone tail, which is black on top and white below. The tail is always less than half but more than one-third of the body length – a feature that helps to distinguish it from the field vole, which has a much shorter tail.

Bank voles occur in large numbers within a small area. Females tend to be unsociable and aggressively defend their territories.

VOLES APART

It is sometimes difficult to tell whether a briefly glimpsed small mammal was a vole or a mouse. More difficult still is distinguishing between the two small vole species found on the British mainland, the bank vole and the field vole.

One obvious difference is the colour of their fur. Bank voles have chestnut fur above and whitish below, while field voles are greyish brown. However, juvenile bank voles are also greyish in colour before their first moult, so this can be confusing.

Another way of identifying the species of vole is from its teeth. This is difficult with a live animal, of course, but voles of both kinds are a favourite food of owls and are often found in their pellets.

Looking at skulls in owl pellets with a hand lens reveals that voles have a zig-zag pattern to the surface of their teeth (mice have knobbly teeth). This helps them to shred tough vegetation. Field voles have very sharply angled teeth while bank vole teeth have more rounded, smoother surfaces.

BANK VOLE FACT FILE

Spring is the best time to watch for this creature, when it may be tempted out from its hideaway to feed on fat buds and blossoming flowers.

● NAMES
Common name: bank vole
Scientific name: *Clethrionomys glareolus*

● HABITAT
Bushes, scrub, hedgerows, plantations and other woodlands; drier areas of reed and sedge beds; sometimes in gardens; rarely in open habitats (unlike field vole)

● DISTRIBUTION
Throughout mainland Britain and many offshore islands; still spreading in Ireland after introduction sometime in the early 1960s

● STATUS
Between 11.5 and 34.5 million individuals at the start of each breeding season

● SIZE
Head and body length about 9–11cm (4in), tail 4–5cm (2in); adult body weight generally 18–25g (⅞oz); fully grown males are around 20% larger than females

● KEY FEATURES
Blunt nose, mainly reddish brown coat, short legs, smallish eyes and small ears

● HABITS
Females defend territories against other females; males are not territorial and their home ranges overlap one another

● VOICE
Various chattering and squeaking sounds; loud squeaks especially during fights; teeth grating and chittering. Males are thought to make ultrasonic calls during fights

● FOOD
Almost entirely vegetable material, especially fruits, nuts, buds and leaves; occasionally insects, worms and snails

● BREEDING
Usually between March and October; litter from 1–7, average 4; young leave nest at around 4 weeks; female has up to 5 or even 6 litters in a season

● NEST
Ball-shaped, made of leaves, moss and feathers in woodland; grass and moss in grassy areas; usually in a chamber off a shallow burrow

● YOUNG
Similar to adults, but smaller and have much greyer fur

● SIGNS
Droppings like those of mice, but smaller than those of woodmouse, four times as long as wide, blackish or dark brown; often deposited in small groups. Hazelnuts gnawed to leave large, smooth-edged circular hole

Although tiny, the bank vole has strong limbs with which to grip small, sometimes slippery fruits – among its favourite food.

Chestnut-coloured fur helps to distinguish the bank vole from the greyish brown field vole.

Long whiskers allow the vole to feel its way around in its burrow.

The bank vole's tail is distinctly dark on top and pale below, unlike the uniform colouring of the field vole.

Distribution map key

Present all year round

Not present

FEEDING HABITS

Fleshy fruits and soft seeds are the staple diet of the bank vole but these are generally available in autumn only. At other times, buds and leaves may be consumed. In winter, even dead leaves will be eaten, despite their lack of nutritious content. Moss, lichens, new roots, flowers and fungi are also taken when they become available, and the odd worm, snail or insect makes an occasional snack. Bank voles often gnaw on bark in winter when other foods are in short supply. This may result in serious damage being done to newly planted trees. Eating seeds and bark can also harm tree regeneration in natural woodlands, so in years when vole populations are high they may be regarded as a pest.

The bank vole forages throughout winter, but some food, particularly nuts and beechmast, is stored away in the burrow system or stashed in hiding places under logs for later use. Bank voles are fond of hazelnuts, which they open in a distinctive way, gnawing a neat hole in one side, with a clean, sharp edge and no obvious visible tooth marks. They also like to eat rose hips, but discard the pips. Since the bank vole's food is often hard and gritty, their teeth tend to get very worn but the molars and incisors continue to grow to compensate for the wear. Only in older animals does tooth growth cease.

Flexible feeding

The success of the bank vole as a species is due in part to its ability to make a meal out of more or less anything it finds. This little mammal often stores some food to help it through winter, but the first buds and flowers of spring make a welcome change from tree bark.

Excursions into the open put the vole at risk from kestrels and owls. Food is therefore often taken underground or to a place of shelter to eat.

A bank vole, unusually caught out in the open, shows the distinctive reddish fur very clearly. They normally make use of surrounding vegetation to hide from potential predators.

Territorial concerns

Bank voles inhabit hedgerows and shrubby areas with dense vegetation, where they usually dig shallow burrow systems a few centimetres below the surface in loose soil or leaf litter. Where the undergrowth is thick enough, they beat a network of tunnels along which they forage at any time of the day or night, although their main periods of activity are around dawn and dusk. In a chamber within the burrow system, the female bank vole constructs a nest using leaves, moss, grass and other soft material collected nearby. Alternatively, she may site the nest in a tree stump, hollow log or other sheltered place.

While bank voles generally remain at or below ground level, they do sometimes climb up into bushes and low trees, where they are occasionally found occupying nestboxes intended for birds or dormice, and in the autumn, they may seek out old thrush and blackbird nests from where they can reach the succulent berries on which they feed.

Bank voles live at high densities – typically there are up to 80 individuals per hectare (2½ acres), but occasionally far more. Females fiercely defend their territories against other females, but males have larger home ranges that overlap those of other males and several females. Sexually mature males can be very aggressive, especially during the breeding season. They fight viciously, often making loud squeaks as they do so. Adult males frequently carry serious bite wounds as a result of these skirmishes. Younger animals and females seem to escape such attacks.

Voles recognise each other using scent, which also plays a part in reproduction – the odour of a strange male can prevent normal pregnancy development in females. The sense of smell may also help voles find their way home. Voles taken from their own territory and released elsewhere can return over considerable distances. Those with their own territories do so more readily than younger voles without an established home.

Raising young

In some years, bank voles may breed during the winter months, but the normal breeding season starts in March and continues until the autumn. Sometimes breeding goes on well into the winter if the weather is favourable and there is plenty of food about. Similarly, breeding can start early in the year in mild conditions. The males develop relatively enormous testes, weighing nearly 5 per cent of their total body weight.

After a pregnancy lasting 18–20 days, females give birth to as many as seven young, although the average family size is four. Babies weigh about 2g (a fraction of an ounce) at birth and are blind and naked. These helpless creatures are suckled by their mother, who has four pairs of teats, for nearly three weeks. The babies emit high-pitched squeaks beyond the range of human hearing and these may help the mother to find and retrieve any that wriggle away from the nest.

After about three days, the first signs of skin pigmentation appear. Fur starts to grow by the eighth day after birth, and covers the upper body completely by the twelfth day, when the eyes and ears open. White underfur appears soon after. The babies grow amazingly fast, are weaned at two weeks old and are soon able to look after themselves. Their teeth are fully in place by four weeks old, when they leave the nest and become independent.

▲ Bank voles are elusive creatures, secreting themselves in shallow underground burrow systems or sheltering among tree stumps for protection from predators and bad weather.

▼ Many small mammals, including bank voles, eat fungi as a valuable extra food source, whenever they are available. Bank voles have to be flexible with their diet to accommodate changing seasons.

▲ Although they spend most of their time on the ground, bank voles do climb up into shrubs and bushes and may sometimes set up home in bird nestboxes.

Berry feast

When the tasty fruits of the hedgerow are abundant, bank voles join in the feast. They nibble away at the flesh of blackberries, leaving the bare core still hanging on the bramble branch.

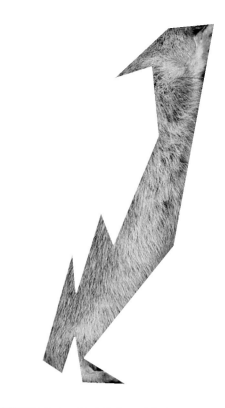

A sensitive quivering nose leads the bank vole to its next meal. In autumn, these voles are spoiled for choice.

Although bank voles usually feed at ground level, they will not be defeated by food that grows higher in the undergrowth.

Despite its very short legs, the bank vole is extremely nimble, especially when it has picked up the scent of a meal.

The young have their first moult at about four to six weeks of age, losing their greyish baby coats, and both male and female juveniles disperse as they reach sexual maturity and adult size.

Boom and bust

Once they have started to breed, females may produce up to five or six litters during the season. Many are able to breed in the same year they were born. This reproduction rate enables the population to build up rapidly and in some years there may be very high numbers of bank voles by late summer – as many as 150 or more per hectare (2½ acres). The low point comes in late winter before breeding starts again, when there may be only five per hectare. Numbers fluctuate widely during the seasons and also from year to year. In some parts of northern Europe, populations peak regularly, but this does not happen in Britain.

Survival rates are low because inexperienced young voles face so many dangers. Over half of those born early in the season die before they are four months old. Those born later fare better, but even so the average life span of the

ISLAND RACES

The bank vole is one of Britain's native mammals, having arrived at the end of the last Ice Age. It is now found throughout the mainland and has also reached many offshore islands thanks to human assistance. Small mammals like this are easily scooped up by accident in fodder for domestic animals, building materials or even with domestic baggage, and taken by boat to islands that they would not have reached unaided.

As a result, there are now bank voles on many of the Scottish and Welsh islands, populations that have been genetically separated from the mainland masses for hundreds of years. In these circumstances, the island animal may undergo a private evolution, developing distinctive forms to be found on that island and nowhere else.

The most distinctive of these peculiar island races is that found on Skomer Island off the south-west coast of Wales. Somehow, bank voles arrived there many generations ago and,

in the absence of other voles, they have evolved to giant size.

Typically, a Skomer vole is about twice the size of a mainland bank vole. The island voles have no mammalian predators to threaten them and they have become very tame – it is even possible to catch them by hand. However, despite the differences, they remain the same species and can interbreed with

mainland bank voles. They live at high densities in the bluebells and bracken that cover Skomer Island, with a total adult population of about 7,000 animals.

Although they are the same species, Skomer voles are about twice the size of mainland bank voles.

▶ Female bank voles usually give birth to an average of four young every four to six weeks during the breeding season. Large numbers of offspring are needed to balance the high juvenile mortality rate.

▲ Grass, along with moss and leaves, is collected for a nest, which is built either underground or in a sheltered spot, hidden from possible predators.

BANK VOLES IN IRELAND

Formerly there were no voles of any species in Ireland, but in 1964 bank voles were reported in the south-west of the country for the first time. It appears that they had arrived accidentally, most likely with imported goods from mainland Britain. Over the following years, they have turned up at increasing distances from their presumed area of introduction, spreading at a rate of about one kilometre (just over half a mile) per year. Ireland is rich in hedgerows and other ideal bank vole habitats, and so it is likely that the species will colonise the whole of Ireland within the next few decades.

WILDLIFE WATCH

Where can I see bank voles?

● Bank voles are common but are unlikely to be seen except by accident. Unfortunately, you are most likely to find dead ones, victims of cats or other predators.

● Bank voles are easily trapped and are sometimes marked and released as part of monitoring programmes. Contact your local Wildlife Trust or Countryside Ranger Service to find out about projects in your area.

● You increase your chances of recognising a bank vole from a fleeting glimpse by being prepared. Rustles in the undergrowth and small tunnels in the grass are clues that something is close by, so keep you eyes peeled and walk quietly.

bank vole is probably less than six months. A few lucky individuals may live more than two years.

The main threats are predators, such as the tawny owl, which may take nearly one third of the whole population in some places, domestic and feral cats, and weasels, which are small enough to enter bank vole burrows and eat both the adults and young.

Other predators range from barn owls to pine martens, stoats and foxes, but in none of these species do bank voles form a major part of the normal diet.

The weather also plays an important part in assisting or preventing survival. Total numbers of voles depend very much on food availability during the previous year and the harshness of the intervening winter.

Balancing act

Bank voles are proficient climbers – they may have been born in a bird's nest – and will clamber along the branches to reach fruits and berries.

The secretive nature of the bank vole means that relatively little is known about their social habits. They lead generally solitary lives, but in the summer a chance encounter in the hawthorn may lead to another litter of young.

The barn owl

Most often glimpsed as a flash in the car headlights on a late-night journey, the barn owl is a highly skilled hunter, although an increasingly rare sight nowadays.

On a fine, warm spring evening, one of the most thrilling sights must be a barn owl gliding silently through the dusk. Often seen near water and above fields and meadows, the barn owl flies slowly and buoyantly back and forth across its hunting ground, constantly watching for movement in the grass below. In spring and summer, both male and female owls are particularly active, since they usually have a brood of hungry chicks not far away.

Barn owls are one of the most characteristic creatures of the British countryside and have successfully adapted to life alongside humans – taking advantage of the nest and roost sites provided by old and abandoned buildings. However, many people may never see one alive in the wild, and changes to the landscape mean they are far less common than they once were.

Hunting for prey

Methodical hunters, barn owls quarter meadows as they fly a few feet above the ground, using their sharp eyesight and hearing to watch and listen for stirrings of prey in the grass. Despite their large eyes and apparent lack of ears, hearing is far more important to the birds' hunting technique than sight. Even the faintest sounds are funnelled into the concealed ears by stiff feathers around the face mask. The ears are not symmetrically positioned on either side of the head and the difference in time between a sound arriving in one ear and in the other allows the owl to work out the exact direction and range of the sound. To make the maximum use of this amazing facility, the wings have developed to keep wind resistance as low as possible, producing a bare minimum of excess noise so as not to confuse the owl's hunting instincts.

When a patrolling barn owl picks up the faint rustlings of a mouse or vole in the vegetation, it rises slightly and slows its flight still further, turning its head to stare in the direction of the noise before diving headlong towards the ground. At the last instant the legs swing forward and the owl plunges, talons spread wide, into the grass and onto its victim.

Life on the edge

With only about 5000 pairs breeding in the British Isles, the barn owl is struggling to survive. Numbers have declined by perhaps 70 per cent in the past half-century. Although they may use buildings as nest sites, barn owls are birds of open

After a successful hunting foray, an adult arrives to feed its young. It will carry its prey in its talons for most of the journey, transferring it to the bill at the nest site.

BARN OWL FACT FILE

A ghostly white appearance and circular face mask ensure the barn owl is unmistakable. From the underside, the bird appears exceptionally pale. It has large, strong wings with soft-edged feathers that enable it to fly noiselessly.

● **NAMES**
Common name: barn owl
Scientific name: *Tyto alba*

● **HABITAT**
Open lowlands, rough grassland, pasture, hedges, banks, ditches and roadside verges

● **DISTRIBUTION**
Lowland areas, predominantly farmland, below 300m (1000ft)

● **STATUS**
Uncommon; estimated 5000 pairs in Britain and Ireland. Major decline due to agricultural practices and 3–5000 road deaths per year

● **SIZE**
Height 33–35cm (13–14in)

● **KEY FEATURES**
White, heart-shaped face with black eyes; mostly white body; head, back and upperside of wings golden-buff with some grey; males generally have fewer markings below

● **HABITS**
Flies mostly from just before sunset until dawn, though also hunts in late afternoon, especially in summer when it has young to feed; from time to time hunts during the day in winter

● **VOICE**
Blood-curdling screeching call, also various hissing, snoring and yapping calls at nest site; young have a loud hissing/snoring call

● **FOOD**
Mainly small mammals – voles, mice, shrews, rats – and also small to medium birds; some catch bats

● **BREEDING**
April or May; not unusual to have a second brood later in year

● **NEST**
Depression in debris of old regurgitated pellets; tree holes, traditional barns and other buildings, nestboxes, holes in cliff faces

● **EGGS**
4–7 round, chalky white eggs laid at intervals of 2–3 days; incubated by female for 30–32 days

● **YOUNG**
Naked at first; soft cover of mainly white down grows after a few days; fledge after 55–65 days

Asymmetrical ears enable the barn owl to pinpoint the direction of sounds with fantastic precision.

The stiff feathers of the facial disc funnel sounds to the bird's sensitive ears.

Although the bird looks large, it has a small body beneath deep, soft feathering.

The owl's fiercely taloned feet are its principal hunting weapons. The outer toe on each foot is reversible to aid the capture of its prey and to keep a firm grip on it in flight.

The serrated leading edge to the wing breaks up the wind-flow and aids silent flight, an essential requirement for a night-hunting predator relying on stealth.

Distribution map key

 Present all year round

☐ Not present

PROTECTED!

The barn owl is afforded special protection under the Wildlife and Countryside Act, Schedule 1. It is an offence to disturb one at the nest without a licence.

How the barn owl hunts

Employing a series of precise movements, the barn owl pinpoints prey with a deliberate search, and the hunt ends in a sudden, dramatic swoop.

Despite its size and pale colour, both of which could attract attention, the barn owl is an expert hunter. It relies upon silence and surprise to catch its prey.

Patrolling from the air, the owl systematically quarters, or ranges over, its hunting territory.

Listening hard as it flies silently along, the owl's keen hearing has picked up the rustling sound of a vole moving about far below.

Although owls are thought of as exclusively nocturnal birds, barn owls often hunt at dusk. In fact, they can sometimes be seen while it is still light, particularly during the summer when the days are long.

countryside, hunting over rough grassland, in weed-infested corners, along roadside verges and railway embankments, and along hedgerows, ditches and river banks. Intensified agriculture means there are fewer and fewer of these untended areas, and a corresponding reduction in the small mammals on which the barn owl feeds. Roads are another danger – although owls rarely collide head-on with vehicles, the wind caused by a speeding lorry can pluck them out of hedgerows and send them tumbling onto the road. Luckily, local water meadows still provide adequate hunting and consequently support a few of these majestic, silent hunters.

Although most hunting occurs only when the sun is below the horizon, in summer, barn owls can sometimes be seen flying before sunset. Both adult birds hunt well before dark to meet the demands of their growing brood. They can also be seen early in the morning, with some birds hunting until perhaps 8 o'clock in undisturbed areas.

During the winter, longer nights give the owls longer to hunt, but bad weather brings problems. The soft plumage, which gives owls such silent flight, can soon become waterlogged and a couple of nights of continuous rain means that they are unable to hunt. Snow cover, or a prolonged, severe frosty spell, encourages voles and mice to spend more time in deeper cover to keep warm. So if it is wet, snowy or very cold, the owls will go

hungry and perhaps even starve. The sight of an owl hunting in the middle of a fine winter's day may be an unexpected pleasure, but it is a sign that the owl is engaged in a desperate fight for survival. Be careful to watch from a good distance, as any disturbance or intrusion could mean that the bird uses up extra energy fleeing and its ability to survive is greatly reduced.

A close encounter with a barn owl reveals the fine detail of its plumage. The neat white feathering of the face and body extends down the legs to the top of its feet. The breast shows black speckles. The back and the upperside of the wings are a rich buff colour, almost rusty, and there is a considerable amount of grey with white flecks. Females can be distinguished from males by their more speckled breast and darker back. Other

identifying features are the darker bars on the main flight feathers of the wings.

Raising a family

Owls nest and mate in spring, and the brood of four to seven eggs is incubated by the female alone for about a month. For at least the first ten days after the earliest chick hatches, the male provides all the food. After that, once the young are covered in enough downy feathers to be able to retain body heat, the female also leaves the nest to hunt.

Because the eggs can hatch at two or three day intervals, the youngest of the brood may be as much as two weeks behind the oldest. Dominated by their older siblings and thus deprived of food for some of the time, the younger chicks' development can be slow. However, if

The strong wings work hard but silently to slow the bird down, while ears and eyes are fixed upon the unsuspecting vole.

The owl brings its wings forward, moves its tail downwards, and begins to hover above the vole, keeping its intended victim firmly in sight.

Hovering takes a lot of energy and, being such a large bird, the owl cannot keep it up for long. The owl has about 20 seconds to decide whether to attack or not.

To lose height as quickly as possible, the owl folds its wings upwards, losing lift and dropping silently out of the sky.

Plunging rapidly towards its prey, the bird's large and powerful talons swing down and forward in readiness to strike.

The owl is still falling in almost total silence, thanks to its soft, noise-muffling feathers. The vole has no warning of the predator's approach as it swoops towards the undergrowth for the kill.

The vole is taken with a force that will probably kill it outright, either by asphyxiation or by puncturing vital organs. It is then carried off in the sharp talons or, if the owl has only a short distance to fly, in the beak. By no means every hunting attempt produces a successful result like this one.

there is sufficient food for them to survive their first few weeks, they will almost certainly fledge in due course.

By their third week, the young need two or more small mammals each per night to enable them to grow at a good rate. The female usually feeds the prey piece by piece to the various young, but if one chick is dominant, it may take a complete mouse or vole and swallow it whole. While this may take a considerable effort, the energy intake is worthwhile.

As time goes on, the parents continue to supply food when weather permits. At seven to eight weeks old, the chicks are fully feathered with just a little down remaining. Now the young become more adventurous and inquisitive, exploring the nest site and peering from the nest entrance at the world beyond. If they are nesting in a tree hole, the young may venture outside to survey the nearby landscape. If surprised by anything they see or if the adults call in alarm, they will rush back into the nest.

The older chicks soon take their first cautious flights and quickly become more adventurous, not only exploring the surrounding tree, but also flying further in the hope of intercepting incoming food brought by their parents. Strangely, the adult avoids the approaching young and dashes past them and into the nest. If food is passed from adult to youngster, it usually happens out of sight among the trees.

▶ Two inquisitive chicks peer out from the safety of their tree hole. The weaker chicks in a brood are fed only when the appetites of their older siblings are satisfied. Younger chicks may die of starvation if there is a shortage of prey.

▼ If the nest is threatened, the male makes an aggressive display, lowering his head and spreading his wings to protect both his mate and the eggs.

Surviving alone
About two weeks after leaving the nest, the youngsters will be encouraged to leave their parents' territory and find a hunting ground of their own. Survival is dependent on the ability to hunt and to find an unoccupied area with good numbers of rodents. Often, they will have to defend their new-found territories. The fittest hold the best, while weak birds are forced to move away and resort to less productive areas. Less than half of the youngsters make it through to the next breeding season.

However, there are grounds for optimism about the barn owl's survival. As long as there are enough nesting sites and enough rough, grassy field margins, hedgerows and other habitats where voles and mice can flourish, the owls can raise perhaps two broods in a year, allowing them to make up their losses.

THE BARN OWL CALENDAR

JANUARY • FEBRUARY

Winter is the time of the highest natural mortality. Numbers of small mammals have declined since the end of the breeding season, making it difficult for the owl to locate enough food, and poor weather can have a disastrous effect on the owl's ability to hunt.

MARCH • APRIL

If there has been a mild winter, the owls will be in good condition and will begin nesting in March. Poor weather can put it back well into April. The nest may be in a tree hole, on a floor, ledge or even a beam in a building. Loss of nesting sites is a major problem, although nestboxes can provide suitable alternatives.

MAY • JUNE

Most females will be incubating their eggs during this period, briefly leaving the nest two or three times a day for a stretch and to relieve themselves. The males provide all sustenance for the pair. When the young hatch, the males will have to provide even more food.

JULY • AUGUST

Chicks should be growing well now. Once they have a covering of down, the female will help with the hunting. If there is a shortage of prey available, the youngest chicks may starve as their older siblings claim most of the food supply.

SEPTEMBER • OCTOBER

All the young should have left the nest by now and will be wandering in search of their own territories. Studies show that most young owls remain fairly close to their parents' territory, but it is during this period that owls may be seen in unexpected locations.

NOVEMBER • DECEMBER

Life again becomes difficult as prey numbers decline and the weather worsens. Adults will have been on individual territories for some time now. It is unusual to see them at the previous summer's nest site.

WILDLIFE WATCH

Where can I see barn owls in the wild?

● Good places to look for barn owls are water meadows and field edges, and rough grassland by rivers, streams, ditches, lakes, hedgerows, roadside verges and set-aside land.

● If you are lucky enough to have a garden that backs on to fields or a river, you may spot an owl very close to home. Quiet and patient waiting, with a pair of binoculars to hand if you have them, may reward you with a sighting of a barn owl.

● Barn owls are a resident species in the British Isles and you may see them at any time of year. The best times of day to see barn owls are just after sunset and just before dawn, but they hunt all through the night and sometimes during the day.

Where can I see captive barn owls?

● Visiting an owl sanctuary is a good way to help owls directly and guarantees that you can see these beautiful creatures close up.

● Most zoos have an owl exhibit, and wildlife rescue centres often have barn owls – some of which are rehabilitated and released, while others may be too badly injured to cope in the wild. The success of 'Harry Potter' has, sadly, created a fad for captive-bred barn owls as pets, and these often end up in rescue centres when their owners discover their mistake.

● In the north of England, a good starting point is the World Owl Trust at The Owl Centre in Ravenglass, Cumbria. Call 01229 717393

● Further south, try the New Forest Owl Sanctuary at Crow, near Ringwood in Hampshire. Call 01425 476487

Recognising buntings

Although they spend most of the year as inconspicuous countryside birds, each spring the male buntings develop handsome breeding plumage in a range of bright colours, which makes them easy to identify.

Many of Britain's smaller birds have adapted to towns and suburbs as human habitation has spread across the land, but some species have resolutely remained birds of countryside alone. Among these are the buntings – small birds, with a superficial resemblance to finches, that

The song of the corn bunting is characteristic of farmland, particularly barley fields, and is often likened to the rattle of a bunch of keys.

are commonly found feeding in flocks on the ground in fields and woodland.

Britain's seven regularly occurring species of bunting belong to a family known as the Emberizidae. They are all well-built birds with short necks, large heads and relatively long tails – the individual species can be recognised and separated more by variations in their plumage than by differences in size and shape.

The structure of the short, conical bill, and of the tongue, is ideally adapted to suit the bird's predominantly seed-eating diet. Buntings will also eat insects at certain times of

the year, especially during the breeding season, and some eat seasonal berries.

Picking them out

Buntings regularly feed in flocks – both with their own species and with other buntings and songbirds. When seen from a distance, there are several ways of distinguishing a bunting from other birds of similar size. The head is smaller than a finch's, and the neck less pronounced. The tail is longer than that of a finch or a sparrow and has only a slight fork at the end – in contrast, most finches have quite a deep tail fork. Feeding habits are also notable, as

buntings feed almost solely on the ground – although they will use fence posts, shrubs and trees as perches. They also nest in trees.

Another way to identify buntings is by their songs, which are composed of simple repeated phrases. Often their calls sound more like dry rattles and jangles than melodious whistles. The songs of finches, on the other hand, have wild, rapidly changing variations, and are very hard to describe.

Bunting breeds

Five species of bunting breed in this country and the other two are regular visitors.

The reed bunting and the brightly coloured yellowhammer are widespread, although their numbers are declining, in their specific habitats of wetlands and farmland. The once-common corn bunting has now become rarc in some areas, although in others it is still seen fairly often. The cirl bunting is extremely scarce and restricted to a few stretches of land in the West Country.

Snow buntings are rare but regular breeding birds of the Scottish mountains – more of them arrive from northern climes in the winter to visit coastal dunes and marshes on the south and east coasts.

The Lapland bunting breeds in Arctic mainland Europe and is a visitor on its way south in autumn – some birds overwinter here. Lastly, the ortolan bunting breeds in mainland Europe and winters in Africa but is an occasional autumn visitor.

In the spring, male reed buntings are easy to spot as they perch prominently near their nests, keeping a wary eye open for danger.

EASY GUIDE TO SPOTTING BUNTINGS

Reed bunting   *Snow bunting*   *Yellowhammer*   *Cirl bunting*

Corn bunting   *Lapland bunting*   *Ortolan bunting*

Distribution map key

- Present all year round
- Present during summer months
- Present during winter months
- Not present

IDENTIFYING BUNTINGS IN NON-BREEDING PLUMAGE

The easiest way to identify buntings is to study males in their spring breeding plumage. However, young birds, non-breeding males and all females are much less distinctive. With careful observation, though, there are several ways to identify these birds as well.

● Reed buntings have well-marked faces in winter, with a pale eyebrow and moustache plus a dark stripe below the moustache. Agitated birds flick their tails nervously revealing white feathers in the outer tail.

● Snow buntings are unmistakable once they take to the wing. The extent of white and black in their wings is unique among coastal songbirds. The bill is pale and dark tipped and the plumage usually suffused with buff on the flanks.

● Yellowhammers almost always appear to have a flush of yellow in their plumage, regardless of the sex of the bird or time of year – females in their first winter are an exception. All birds also show a reddish brown rump and lower back.

● Cirl buntings can appear superficially similar to yellowhammers outside the breeding season, but have a grey-brown rump and lower back with a hint of olive-grey around the neck. Their limited distribution is another important clue.

● Corn buntings are the drabbest and most uniform of all buntings. Their plumage remains essentially the same – rather like that of a skylark – throughout the year. Look for the proportionately large, stubby bill and notice the legs, which often dangle in flight.

● Lapland buntings are superficially similar to non-breeding reed buntings but have a chestnut panel on their wings and a distinctive dry, rattling flight call.

● Ortolan buntings show a warm pinkish buff tone to their plumage. They have a pale yellowish moustache stripe and a pinkish bill.

WILDLIFE WATCH

Where can I see buntings?

● Reed buntings are always associated with wetland areas during the breeding season, particularly reedbeds and patches of bushes and scrub on their margins. In winter, they often form roving flocks which feed on adjacent areas of arable land, sometimes mixing with yellowhammers and chaffinches.

● Snow buntings form flocks outside the breeding season and frequent coastal grassland, both on dunes and headlands. For the best chances of seeing the species, visit the East Anglian coast – particularly north Norfolk – between October and March. The birds are often very approachable, but when they take to the air it becomes immediately obvious why they are nicknamed 'snowflakes' – there is a lot of white in their wings.

● Yellowhammers are generally associated with hedgerows and areas of scrub on dry ground; hawthorn and gorse

are particularly popular. Outside the breeding season, this species forms flocks that mix freely with other buntings and finches.

● Cirl buntings are seldom seen outside their remaining haunts in south-west Britain. For the best chances of seeing them, visit south Devon and walk the coastal path between Plymouth and Torquay in the spring when males will be singing their monotonous songs. Outside the breeding season, the birds form small flocks that feed on arable land, but they seldom wander far from their breeding territories.

● Corn buntings are easiest to see in the spring and early summer on areas of arable farmland, especially on chalk downs. Males often sing while perched on fence posts or wires. Outside the breeding season, corn buntings form flocks, which sometimes mix with

yellowhammers in areas of good feeding – although the birds seldom stray far from suitable breeding terrain.

● Lapland buntings can be found in small flocks on coastal arable land in East Anglia and north Kent in most years, but are more usually encountered as autumn passage migrants. Places such as the Scilly Isles and the north Norfolk coast offer the best chances to see this species.

● Ortolan buntings are seen only as autumn passage migrants. They stop in a particular location, often for just a few hours. Watch the weather forecast for predictions of south-easterly winds in September and then head for migration spots on the south coast, searching newly ploughed fields for these unobtrusive birds. Portland in Dorset, Beachy Head in Sussex and Sandwich Bay in Kent have records of ortolans in most autumns.

REED BUNTING *Emberiza schoeniclus*

As their name suggests, reed buntings tend to favour the margins of reedbeds and marshes, although they have also colonised many drier places. The breeding male has a black and white head with white moustache stripe and broad white collar. The rest of its upperparts are brown with darker streaks, apart from a grey rump. Females have brown, streaked heads with buff eyebrows and moustache. Juveniles resemble females, but have faint head markings.

Reed bunting nests are sited in dense vegetation where the noisy chicks are less conspicuous to potential predators.

Insects form the major part of the diet of reed bunting chicks. Both the male and female (seen here) help feed the brood.

● SIZE
Length 15cm (6in)

● NEST
Substantial cup of grass and moss concealed among ground cover

● BREEDING
Lays 4–5 very pale olive to lilac-grey eggs, mottled purplish black, in April–May

● FOOD
Invertebrates and seeds

● HABITAT
Grassy margins of wetlands; also in farm crops and grasslands

● VOICE
Plaintive '*tseeu*' call on descending scale, and metallic '*ching*'; song simple, repetitive metallic '*tweek, tweek, tweek, tzikky tweek*'

● DISTRIBUTION
Widespread but declining resident across all of Britain and Ireland

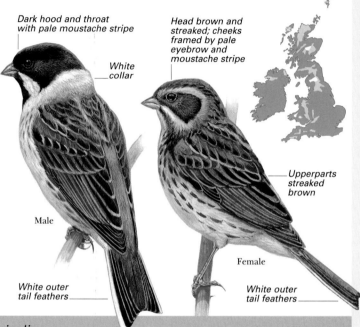

Dark hood and throat with pale moustache stripe

White collar

Head brown and streaked; cheeks framed by pale eyebrow and moustache stripe

Male

White outer tail feathers

Upperparts streaked brown

Female

White outer tail feathers

SNOW BUNTING *Plectrophenax nivalis*

Breeding male snow buntings are easily recognised by their bold black and white plumage and black bill, eyes and legs. Females in summer are brown whereas males are black, with an orange tinge to the white parts of the plumage. In autumn and winter, the plumage of both sexes is browner, the bill is yellow, and cap and cheeks show an orange-buff tinge. Juveniles are browner overall. Flying birds show large patches of white on the wings and tail.

● SIZE
Length 16–17cm (6½in)

● NEST
Cup of grass, moss and lichens in rock crevice

● BREEDING
Lays 4–6 pale bluish or greenish eggs with reddish brown to purplish black blotches in late May–June

● FOOD
Seeds and invertebrates

● HABITAT
Arctic tundra, high mountain plateaux; overwinters on coastal grasslands, saltmarshes, among sand dunes, on shingle beaches

● VOICE
Soft, rippling flight calls and pleasant, loud, fluty trilling song

● DISTRIBUTION
Winter visitor to coasts, mainly in south and east, very scarce breeding bird in northern Scotland; 70–100 pairs currently breed

Juvenile

Colours more subdued than on winter adult birds

Yellow bill

Buff on nape and cheeks

Winter male

Dark legs and feet

White wing patch

Snow buntings show a marked variation in their appearance throughout the year and between the sexes. Breeding males (above left) are essentially black and white, while autumn and winter birds (left) have some buffish yellow and brown in their plumage.

YELLOWHAMMER *Emberiza citrinella*

Adult male yellowhammers in spring and summer are unmistakably colourful, with very bright lemon-yellow heads and chestnut rumps. The upperparts are brown, streaked with black and dark brown, and the underparts are dull yellow with a darker chestnut wash on the breast. Females are much duller with greyish green streaks on the head and chest – but their chestnut rump shows clearly in flight. Juveniles are very similar to females and non-breeding males, but sometimes show very little yellow. The distinctive song of the male is heard through the summer.

● **SIZE**
Length 16–16.5cm (6½in)

● **NEST**
Bulky cup of grass, straw and moss low down in grass clump

● **BREEDING**
Lays 3–5 whitish to pale pinkish eggs with a few dark spots and scribbles in April–May

● **FOOD**
Seeds, some invertebrates in summer

● **HABITAT**
Farmland, hedgerows, heathland, coastal scrub

● **VOICE**
Main call a sharp, brief, metallic '*tzit*'. Rasping song described as '*a-little-bit-of-bread-and-no-cheese*'

● **DISTRIBUTION**
Widespread and fairly common, but declining, resident across mainland Britain and Ireland

The yellowhammer's chestnut rump is obvious in all plumages. This bird is an adult male in summer plumage.

Yellow tinge to head

Female

Male's brilliant lemon-yellow head is particularly striking in spring and summer

Underparts streaked and show yellowish wash

Male

CIRL BUNTING *Emberiza cirlus*

Similar to the yellowhammer in size, shape and behaviour, the breeding male cirl bunting has a yellowish head with bold black eye stripe and chin. His upperparts are chestnut, apart from a dark tail and flight feathers and a grey-brown rump. Underparts have a greenish hue and are not as bright as the male yellowhammer's. Females resemble washed-out males and lack the head markings – the breast is darkly streaked and the rump is olive-grey. Juveniles are a buff-brown version of females.

● **SIZE**
Length 15.5cm (6in)

● **NEST**
Tidy cup of moss, grass and leaves concealed low down in cover

● **BREEDING**
Lays 3–4 greyish white eggs with dark brown spots and scribbles in May

● **FOOD**
Seeds, some insects

● **HABITAT**
Mainly farmland; open, partly wooded locations, gorse-covered slopes, hedgerows

● **VOICE**
Rattling, metallic tuneless song

● **DISTRIBUTION**
Declined since 1930s – by 1989 only 250 birds, all in south Devon; farmland management less damaging to wildlife has led to numbers rising to over 900 by 1998

◄ Adult male cirl buntings have smart and distinctive plumage. The pattern on the head is especially bold.

► Female cirl buntings are rather drab compared with their partners. The grey-brown rump is easy to see only in flying birds.

Streaked brown plumage with grey-brown rump

Female

Yellow eyebrow and yellow on cheeks

Black throat and eye stripe

Greenish breast band

Underparts buff-yellow and streaked on flanks

Olive-grey on nape

Male

Grassland watch

CORN BUNTING *Miliaria calandra*

A large, compact bunting with very plain and unremarkable plumage, the corn bunting's upperparts are buff-brown, streaked with dark brown and black. The underparts are paler and heavily streaked on the breast. The bill is large and pinkish, the eye big and dark, and the legs vary from pinkish to straw-yellow. Males and females are similar. Juveniles are paler, brighter and more yellowish than adults with fewer streaks on their flanks.

● **SIZE**
Length 18cm (7in)

● **NEST**
Untidy cup of grasses and leaves on ground in sparse cover

● **BREEDING**
Lays 3–5 pale blue or buff eggs with dark markings in April–May

● **FOOD**
Seeds and invertebrates

● **HABITAT**
Dry, open farmland with hedgerows; downland, coastal scrub

● **VOICE**
Short, rasping 'chit' contact call, loud, low 'quit' flight call; song a discordant, accelerating series of jangling notes

● **DISTRIBUTION**
Has undergone massive declines since 1960s. Now mainly scattered in east, and in Hebrides and Orkney; very rare in Ireland

Bill proportionately large and stubby

Throat is pale but marked with dark streaks at sides

Plumage essentially brown and faintly streaked

Corn buntings frequently use perches such as fence posts, wires and bare twigs as song posts and also as lookouts when returning to the nest with a bill full of caterpillars.

LAPLAND BUNTING *Calcarius lapponicus*

A well-marked bird, the Lapland bunting shows considerable plumage variation between sexes and throughout the year. The breeding male is unmistakable, its head largely black except for a yellowish cream stripe behind the eye, a chestnut nape and a white collar. Underparts are pale and upperparts streaked brown. Breeding females and all birds outside the breeding season have streaked chestnut-brown upperparts and pale underparts.

● **SIZE**
Length 15.5cm (6in)

● **NEST**
Does not breed in British Isles

● **BREEDING**
Does not breed in British Isles

● **FOOD**
Seeds and invertebrates

● **HABITAT**
Breeds in Arctic tundra and heath; winters in coastal grassland, saltmarshes

● **VOICE**
Calls include a fast, dry, rattling 'tick-tick-tick-it'

● **DISTRIBUTION**
Scarce winter visitor, from late August to mid-May, mainly to eastern coast

Adult male Lapland buntings are rarely seen in breeding plumage in this country, but occasionally turn up on the east coast in May, during their migration.

Chestnut nape seen in all birds

Chestnut panel on wings

Yellowish bill

Autumn male

ORTOLAN BUNTING *Emberiza hortulana*

The seldom-seen breeding male of this subtly marked species has a blue-grey head and neck with a pale lemon-yellow throat and moustache stripe. Its upperparts are streaked reddish brown and its underparts are an unmarked orange-brown. Breeding females and all non-breeding birds are similar, with a grey-brown head, pale yellow throat and moustache stripe. Migrant birds feed unobtrusively, often concealing themselves in furrows on the ground.

● **SIZE**
Length 16cm (6½in)

● **NEST**
Does not breed in British Isles

● **BREEDING**
Does not breed in British Isles

● **FOOD**
Seeds and invertebrates

● **HABITAT**
Migrants usually found on coastal stubble fields and offshore islands

● **VOICE**
Liquid 'tlip' and shrill 'tsee-up' calls

● **DISTRIBUTION**
Rare but regular autumn visitor to coastal and island migration 'hot-spots'

Pinkish bill

Yellowish throat and stripe

Pale eye ring

Ortolan buntings are smart birds with conspicuous pale eye rings and pale moustache stripes. The combination of blue-grey head and reddish brown body plumage is distinctive.

Upperparts reddish brown and streaked

Underparts reddish brown

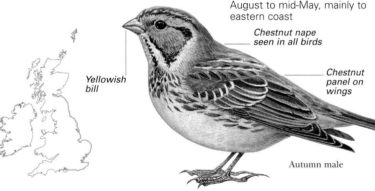

The dung beetle

Animal dung – especially that of cattle and other herbivores – can be a rich source of nutrition for any creature able to tackle it. Britain's wide range of dung beetles is one group of insects that specialise in doing just that.

A single cow can produce a dozen cowpats in a day – enough to smother 200 square metres (240 square yards) of pasture in a year, were it not for the industrious animals that help break the waste down and clear it away. Flies swarm around to lay their eggs in dung while it is still cooling, but dung beetles play the more important role, although they are less conspicuous and do most of their work beneath the ground or under cover of darkness.

Feeding on dung throughout their lives, some dung beetles can consume their own weight every day. The smaller ones, including more than 40 *Aphodius* species, normally feed and breed in the dung where it falls, but the common dor beetle and other large species collect and bury the dung before laying their eggs on it. Under the ground, the grubs are relatively safe from predators and the dung remains moist for a longer period.

At up to 26mm (1in) long, the common dor beetle is one of the largest dung beetles. The wing-cases, or elytra, are black with a blue or green tinge and the underside is metallic blue or green.

This 'green and pleasant land' would be neither were it not for the hard work of dung beetles and other oft-maligned insects in clearing away the waste that larger animals liberally scatter over the landscape.

Industrious dumbledor

The common dor beetle, *Geotrupes stercorarius* – also known as the dumbledor or shardborne – is the most common of six very similar beetles associated with cowpats and other dung, including the widespread *Geotrupes spiniger*, and the wood dor beetle *Geotrupes stercorosus*, often abundant in wooded areas. Few dor beetles are free from infestation by tiny brown mites, which are related to spiders, on their underside, but the beetle's tough outer skeleton protects it from any predators smaller than a fox or badger.

The mites give rise to another common name – the lousy watchman. The 'watchman' part is said to derive from the beetle's habit of flying at dusk, searching for fresh dung with its clubbed antennae at about the time when night watchmen went on their rounds. But although most often on the wing at dusk, when they sometimes crash into cars and lighted windows, common dor beetles fly at any hour of day or night, and the loud rustling of their wings can be alarming.

When two beetles of opposite sexes meet, they quickly mate and begin preparing a home for their offspring. The female uses her spiky front legs and powerful jaws to burrow beneath the dung to depths that may reach 60cm (24in). She constructs four or five small chambers at the end of the burrow, fills them with dung brought down by the male and lays an egg in each chamber. The parent beetles then leave, perhaps to make another burrow under another cowpat. Concealed in burrows, their offspring have a good chance of survival, so dung beetles do not need to produce large numbers of eggs.

A DUNG BEETLE LOOKALIKE

The bloody-nosed beetle (Timarcha tenebricosa), commonly found wandering over grazed turf, is plump and black and, at first sight, resembles the dung beetle, for which it is often mistaken.

Closer inspection, however, reveals significant differences: dung beetle antennae are short and clubbed, while those of the bloody-nosed beetle are quite long and shaped like a string of beads. Look also at the wing cases and the feet – the bloody-nosed beetle has ungrooved elytra and broad, flat feet.

This clumsy, flightless beetle is in fact a leaf-eater and gets its name from its reflex bleeding – the emission of a drop of red blood from its mouth when it is alarmed. This habit is believed to deter would-be predators.

A robust, slow-moving insect, the bloody-nosed beetle is an apparently easy target for insectivorous birds. However, the drop of blood it secretes when attacked is distasteful to predators, and they learn to leave it well alone.

▼ The sturdy wing cases of the common dor beetle are clearly ridged from front to back. In flight, the wings make a droning sound as they beat strongly, keeping the beetle's heavy body aloft.

▲ The common dor and the minotaur beetle belong to the family Geotrupidae, in which powerful jaws are always clearly visible from above. The antennae in this family have distinctive brush-like tips.

RELATED SCARABS

Scarab beetles are most abundant in tropical areas and, apart from the English scarab Copris lunaris, just eight species have been found in the British Isles in small, specific areas. They all belong to the genus Onthophagus. The head is narrower than the thorax, the wing cases are either dull black or brownish and they are never more than 12mm (½in) long.

These scarabs use various kinds of dung, which they normally install in burrows like those of the common dor beetle and the minotaur, but they do not exhibit the parental care shown by English scarabs. Onthophagus coenobita, which can be recognised by its yellowish wing cases and green or coppery thorax, is unusual in making a simple vertical burrow in which it stores several dung balls stacked one on top of the other. It can be found in Wales and the southern half of England from May to July.

◄ Female minotaur beetles use their powerful jaws and legs to dig deep tunnels in light, well-drained soil. Off the main shaft of the tunnel, a female will dig several brood chambers to be filled with dung.

▲ Male minotaur beetles diligently search out and collect the droppings of rabbits and sheep. The male will carefully roll or drag these backwards to the burrow, holding the dung in its two front legs.

Each larva feeds in its own larder for many months and new adult beetles emerge during the following spring or summer. Nevertheless, the burrow does not afford the insects absolute protection. The larvae of various small *Aphodius* species, which normally live in dung on the surface of the ground, sometimes invade the tunnels of the common dor and other *Geotrupes* species to feed on the buried dung masses. They may eat the

eggs and young larvae of *Geotrupes* if they come across them, but otherwise merely steal some of their food. Some common dor beetles are only about 15mm (⅝in) long, and these may well have been those deprived of their normal food intake by an invasion of *Aphodius*.

The other five *Geotrupes* species, mainly differing in the detailed decoration of the thorax and horny wing cases called elytra, have very similar life histories.

Team effort

The minotaur beetle, *Typhaeus typhoeus*, grows up to 20mm (¾in) long and inhabits heathlands and well-grazed grasslands, including coastal cliffs. It is most likely to be seen towards dusk. Males and females work together to excavate a burrow as much as 150cm (60in) deep, although the male, in common with most other beetles with prominent horns, does not do much digging. His job is to get rid of the soil excavated by the female and to haul the dung into the burrow.

The lower end of the burrow leads into several small chambers that are stocked with dung. An egg is laid in the soil close to each chamber and the parent beetles then abandon the nest. All kinds of dung may be used, but sheep and rabbit

The minotaur beetle got its name from the bull-like horns on the male's thorax, which bring to mind the bull-headed beast of ancient legend. There are three horns altogether – two long ones that protrude well beyond the head on each side and a shorter one in the middle. The female has three short horns.

droppings seem to be preferred – although this is probably due to the fact that sheep and rabbits are more common than cattle on the sandy soils and short turf where the minotaur beetles live.

The dung is usually buried where it falls, but if the underlying ground is particularly hard, the beetles may transport it to a softer spot. It has been suggested that the males trundle rabbit droppings along with their horns, but there is no real evidence for this. The beetles have been seen manipulating droppings with their horns, but once on the move they drag it backwards using their strong legs.

Male beetles use their horns to wrestle each other, in the manner of stag beetles, for the right to mate with a female. These fights may take place above or below ground, but when an intruder enters an occupied burrow, the resident male usually wins.

Caring parent

The English scarab, *Copris lunaris*, also known as the horned dung beetle, is very rare, if not extinct, in Britain. It was last found in any numbers in Surrey in 1948, with only a few individuals recorded in later years. Up to 20mm (¾in) long, it is very shiny, with clearly ribbed elytra. Both sexes have a single horn sticking up from the middle of the head shield, although the female's is quite short. The male also has upward-pointing spikes on each side of the thorax and these are used primarily to do battle over females.

This beetle favours well-drained, unploughed pastures and breeds mainly in cow dung that it drags into burrows beneath the cowpats in spring and early summer. As with the minotaur beetle,

males and females share the work, the female doing the digging and the male using his broad head shield to shovel soil out of the burrow and into a spoil heap at the side of the cowpat. When idle, the male may rest at the mouth of the burrow to prevent other males from entering.

The burrow ends in an oval chamber, up to 15cm (6in) in diameter, but only about 5cm (2in) high. Here, the female moulds dung into several pear-shaped masses. She lays an egg in each and stays on hand until her offspring are ready to leave about three months later. After feeding on any dung not used to make the 'pears', she fasts for the rest of the time that she is in the nest.

Her presence deters parasites and other enemies, and by regularly licking and turning the 'pears' she reduces the possibility of mould damage to both dung

The strong legs of the common dor beetle are armed with spines and 'teeth' that aid the process of dragging a heavy dung ball over the ground to the nursery burrow.

and larvae. This high degree of parental care allows the beetle to get away with laying very few eggs – rarely more than five in a nest. The male usually leaves as soon as the burrow has been fully stocked.

The English scarab has probably always been on the edge of its range in the British Isles and confined mainly to the southern counties of England. Its decline and possible extinction can be linked to the withdrawal of grazing animals from downland and the subsequent ploughing of many areas. Droughts have also been implicated in the decline, by drying out the ground and making it more difficult for the beetles to burrow.

WILDLIFE WATCH

Where can I find dung beetles?

● Look in fields and pastures containing grazing animals. Turn over dried cowpats and other dung to find the burrows – be sure to replace the cowpat afterwards. The beetles are most active from spring to late autumn. They fly mainly at dusk or at night and can sometimes be attracted by a powerful torch or car headlights.

● Dor beetles can be found throughout the British Isles. Minotaurs occur in England and Wales, more commonly in the south. The English scarab is unlikely to be seen, but other scarabs may be found in southern England.

Most common dor beetles are infested with tiny brown mites that live on fluids sucked from the soft underside. Although there may be dozens of them, the mites do not seem to harm the beetles.

Wild grasses

Many different species of grass proliferate in Britain. Some are cultivated or used to seed waste ground, but the landscape would be immeasurably poorer without the beauty of wild grasses in meadows and pastures.

Whether natural or planted, grasses of one sort or another combine to form the dominant plant cover in much of the British Isles. They are all wind-pollinated flowering plants, members of the family Gramineae, and are most noticeable in spring and early summer, as they flower on waysides and in meadows and pastures. Most native grasses bloom in June and July. The flowers are tiny, green and usually grouped in small clusters. The shape of the flower clusters varies from species to species, which helps in identification. They may be narrow and spiky, or loosely branched. The flower parts are merely green or yellowish papery scales, with male stamens on long, loose stalks. The fruits are single-seeded, with the starch-rich seed covered in a papery husk.

Green at first, the husk ripens to a brown or yellowish colour.

Most grasses have rhizomes – underground stems bearing scale-like leaves – and runners that creep along the ground, occasionally rooting and putting out new shoots.

Perennial grasses are a traditional crop. Meadows and grazing pastures covered much of the country for a long time, supporting a wealth of wildlife, but 95 per cent of this 'unimproved' farm grassland has vanished since 1945. It survives on only a few farms today. Pastures have been ploughed up for arable land or temporary grassland. In many areas, silage – grass cut and stored while green – has replaced hay.

Green future

Nevertheless, wild grasses are a valuable resource. Related to modern agricultural grasses and to the amenity grasses used in lawns and for roadside verges, their genetic diversity is important to plant breeders. Some are also useful for reclaiming marginal land – for instance, marram grass is widely used to bind eroding sand dunes, and steep slopes can be stabilised by red fescue and ryegrass, among others. Today, the last of the old meadows are protected habitats and efforts are under way to help re-establish diverse grasslands elsewhere.

Britain's ancient hay meadows are among the most rigorously managed of habitats. Yet they retain a rich mix of flowers and grasses that are reminiscent of wild, natural grasslands.

Like other grasses, cock's-foot releases its pollen into the air. It is then carried on the breeze until it is trapped by the feather-like female stigmas.

WILD GRASS FACT FILE

● Common salt marsh grass, sea meadow grass or sea poa
Puccinellia maritima
Habitat and distribution
Common in wetter salt-marsh turf; colonises bare mud, sometimes sand and rocks; throughout the British Isles
Size 10–80cm (4–32in) tall
Key features
Densely tufted, with numerous long runners and spreading stems; flowers in branched groups of cylindrical clusters; leaves narrow, stiff
Flowering time
June–July

● Sand couch grass or sand twitch grass
Elytrigia juncea
Habitat and distribution
Common at top of sandy beaches and in unconsolidated sand dunes throughout British Isles
Size 20–60cm (8–24in) tall
Key features
Loosely tufted, with far-creeping rhizomes and brittle stems; flowers in stout spikes 4–20cm (1½–8in) long; leaves tightly rolled, bluish or greyish green
Flowering time
June–August

● Common cord-grass or rice-grass
Spartina anglica
Habitat and distribution
Abundant on mudflats and in salt-marsh pools, mainly in southern Britain and Ireland
Size 30–130cm (12–51in) tall
Key features
Clump-forming, with stout, fleshy, far-creeping rhizomes and stout stems; flowers in 2–12 cylindrical spikes up to 25cm (10in) long; leaves yellowish green or greyish green
Flowering time
July–November

● Marram grass
Ammophila arenaria
Habitat and distribution
Common on sand dunes, sometimes on sandy cliffs and shingle, throughout British Isles
Size 50–120cm (20–48in) tall
Key features
Densely tufted, with stout, far-creeping rhizomes and stiff stems; flowers in cylindrical, spike-like clusters up to 25cm (10in) long; leaves grey-green, sharply pointed, edges rolled inward
Flowering time
June–August

● Timothy grass or meadow cat's-tail
Phleum pratense
Habitat and distribution
Common in old or newly sown meadows and pastures, and on hill grassland, roadsides, wasteland, throughout British Isles except Highlands of Scotland and parts of Ireland
Size 40–150cm (16–60in) tall
Key features
Tufted, with slender or stout stems; flowers in dense, stiff, cylindrical spikes, 2–20cm (1–8in) long; leaves green or greyish green
Flowering time
June–September

● Reed canary grass
Phalaris arundinacea
Habitat and distribution
Common beside watercourses, in fens and damp grassy areas; often forms large patches; throughout British Isles
Size 60–200cm (24–80in) tall
Key features
Robust, with far-creeping rhizomes and stout, leafy stems; flowers in dense, spreading, often purplish or whitish clusters
Flowering time
June–August

Common salt marsh grass, sea meadow grass or sea poa
Puccinellia maritima

Common cord-grass or rice-grass
Spartina anglica

Sand couch grass or sand twitch grass
Elytrigia juncea

Timothy grass or meadow cat's-tail
Phleum pratense

Reed canary grass
Phalaris arundinacea

Marram grass
Ammophila arenaria

The silky heads of Timothy grass adorn roadsides, field margins and waste ground throughout Britain. This handsome grass is grown extensively for grazing and hay.

WILD GRASS FACT FILE

● False (or tall) oat-grass
Arrhenatherum elatius
Habitat and distribution
Common in rough grassland on field margins, roadsides, wasteland and shingle beaches throughout British Isles
Size 50–200cm (20–80in) tall
Key features
Loosely tufted, with stout stems, often with onion-like swellings at base; flowers whiskered in long, loose, short-branched clusters; leaves coarse
Flowering time
May–September

● Meadow (or common) foxtail
Alopecurus pratensis
Habitat and distribution
Common, especially in moist grassland, throughout the British Isles
Size 30–120cm (12–48in) tall
Key features
Tufted, with slender stems; flowers early in dense, soft, cylindrical spikes, up to 10cm (4in) long, loosely covered in withered red-brown stamens
Flowering time
April–June

● Perennial ryegrass
Lolium perenne
Habitat and distribution
Common in grassland, meadows, pastures, also on verges, wasteland, throughout British Isles
Size 10–90cm (4–36in) tall
Key features
Loosely tufted, with rather stiff stems; flowers in numerous flattened clusters along the stem; leaves shiny, bright green
Flowering time
May–November

● Sweet vernal grass
Anthoxanthum odoratum
Habitat and distribution
Widespread in all grassland, especially old meadows and pastures, throughout British Isles
Size 10–100cm (4–40in) tall
Key features
Tufted, with rather stiff stems; flowers early, in fairly dense spikes up to 12cm (5in) long; bright green leaves, fragrant when bruised; smells of new-mown hay when dried
Flowering time
April–July

● Crested dog's tail
Cynosurus cristatus
Habitat and distribution
Common in grassland, especially old pastures, even on poor, dry soils throughout British Isles
Size 5–75cm (2–30in) tall
Key features
Tufted, with slender stems; flowers in dense, stiff, single-sided, spikes up to 14cm (5½in) long; leaves narrow
Flowering time
June–August

● Cock's-foot
Dactylis glomerata
Habitat and distribution
Common in pastures and rough grassland, on roadsides and seaside cliffs throughout British Isles
Size 20–130cm (8–51in) tall
Key features
Coarse, densely tufted, with rough stems; flowers in large, dense, single-sided clusters; leaves broad, 'V'-shaped in section, often greyish green
Flowering time
June–October

Sweet vernal grass cloaks heaths, moors, hill grassland and open woodlands with a fresh green. It flowers early and smells strongly of cut grass.

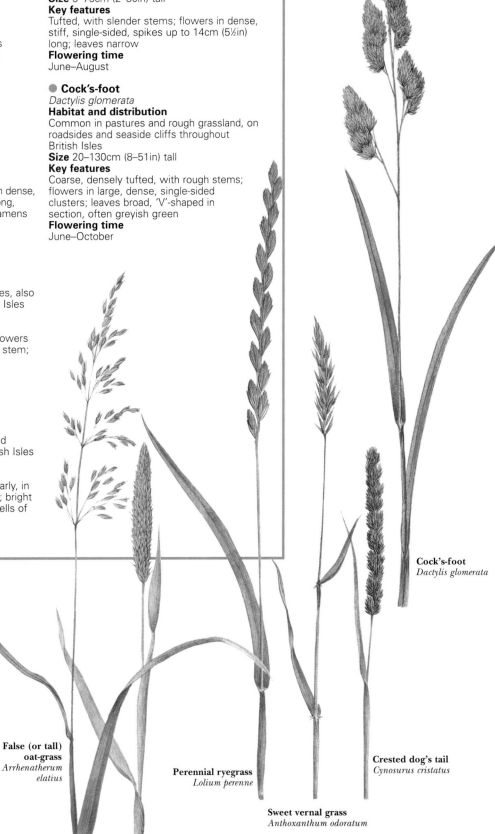

Cock's-foot
Dactylis glomerata

False (or tall) oat-grass
Arrhenatherum elatius

Perennial ryegrass
Lolium perenne

Crested dog's tail
Cynosurus cristatus

Sweet vernal grass
Anthoxanthum odoratum

Meadow (or common) foxtail
Alopecurus pratensis

Quaking grass is very distinctive, with heads of loosely hung, heart-shaped spikelets. These tremble in the slightest breeze and have inspired numerous descriptive local names such as totter grass and dithery dock.

WILD GRASS FACT FILE

● **Red fescue or creeping fescue**
Festuca rubra
Habitat and distribution
Widespread in well-drained grassland, including sand dunes, salt marshes and lawns throughout British Isles
Size 10–100cm (4–40in) tall
Key features
Loosely tufted, with slender rhizomes, wiry stems; reddish, purplish, or greenish flowers in loosely branched groups of flattened clusters; leaves narrow, each with reddish sheath at base, completely closed when young; can be bluish, especially on coasts
Flowering time
May–July

● **Sheep's fescue**
Festuca ovina
Habitat and distribution
Widespread in grassland on poor, well-drained soils, especially in uplands, throughout British Isles
Size 5–60cm (2–24in) tall
Key features
Similar to red fescue, but densely tufted, without rhizomes; flowers more compact; less reddish leaves at base; sheaths split more than halfway
Flowering time
May–July

● **Common bent or fine bent**
Agrostis capillaris
Habitat and distribution
Common in grassland on well-drained, poorer acid soils, especially in uplands, throughout British Isles
Size 10–70cm (4–28in) tall
Key features
Tufted, with short rhizomes and runners and wiry stems; flowers in diffuse, branched clusters; individual flowers; leaves narrow
Flowering time
Late June–August

● **Creeping bent**
Agrostis stolonifera
Habitat and distribution
Common in pastures, marshes and sand dunes, on downs and other grasslands, roadsides and as a garden weed, throughout British Isles
Size 8–40cm (3–16in) tall
Key features
Similar to common bent, but with far-creeping, leafy runners; flowers densely clustered; leaves greyish green
Flowering time
July–August

● **Meadow oat-grass**
Helictotrichon pratense
Habitat and distribution
Often abundant in short grassland, mainly on chalk or limestone; widespread in Britain, absent from Ireland
Size 30–80cm (12–32in) tall
Key features
Densely tufted, with stiff, slender stems; bluish green leaves; flowers whiskered, in loose clusters, in groups of 1–2 on short branches
Flowering time
June–July

● **Common quaking grass or totter grass**
Briza media
Habitat and distribution
Widespread in grassland on lime-rich soils, especially chalk, throughout most of British Isles
Size 15–75cm (6–30in) tall
Key features
Loosely tufted, with short rhizomes and wiry stems; flowers in distinctive, loose, usually purplish pyramidal clusters, individual groups oval and flattened
Flowering time
May–August

Red fescue or creeping fescue
Festuca rubra

Sheep's fescue
Festuca ovina

Common bent or fine bent
Agrostis capillaris

Creeping bent
Agrostis stolonifera

Meadow oat-grass
Helictotrichon pratense

Common quaking grass or totter grass
Briza media

Like other members of the fescue family, red fescue is a very useful and important grass of chalky soils. The many cultivated varieties also make excellent lawn grasses.

WILD GRASS FACT FILE

● **Upright brome**
Bromopsis erecta
Habitat and distribution
Common in chalk and limestone grassland, especially in southern and central England
Size 40–120cm (16–48in) tall
Key features
Densely tufted, coarse, with stiff stems; flowers in loose, erect clusters; groups spear-shaped, flattened, sometimes purplish
Flowering time
May–July

● **Tor grass or chalk false-brome**
Brachypodium rupestre
Habitat and distribution
Abundant in places in grassland on chalk and limestone, mainly in southern England
Size 30–120cm (12–48in) tall
Key features
Tufted, coarse, with stiff stems; flowers in loose, erect, spiky yellowish green clusters
Flowering time
June–August

● **Smooth meadow grass**
Poa pratensis
Habitat and distribution
Common on well-drained soils, meadows and pastures, and on roadsides throughout British Isles
Size 10–90cm (4–36in) tall
Key features
Loosely tufted, with slender rhizomes; flowers in neat, branched groups of flattened clusters 4–6mm (⅛–¼in) long; leaves rather blunt, mid-green
Flowering time
Late April–early July

● **Rough meadow grass**
Poa trivialis
Habitat and distribution
Common in grassland on rich, moist soils often in partial shade, throughout the British Isles
Size 20–100cm (8–40in) tall
Key features
Similar to smooth meadow-grass but with leafy, creeping runners; flower clusters 3–4mm (⅛in) long; rough leaves near base; leaves paler green than smooth meadow grass, with slightly rough sheaths
Flowering time
June–July

The loosely tufted, light green leaves of tor grass frequently invade chalk downland turf, forming vast blankets of rippling grass. The species is usually avoided by grazing cattle.

Tor grass or chalk false-brome
Brachypodium rupestre

Smooth meadow grass
Poa pratensis

Rough meadow grass
Poa trivialis

Upright brome
Bromopsis erecta

WILDLIFE WATCH

Where do wild grasses grow?

● The best places to find a variety of species are old meadows and pastures, watersides, dry roadside banks and grassy heaths.

● Some grasses are characteristic of specific habitats. For instance, look on chalk or limestone soils for upright brome and tor grass, and on sand dunes, shingle beaches or in salt marshes for marram grass.

Golden dandelions

Found in almost every habitat, these cheerful, prolific flowers enliven many a dull roadside or grassy space. They may all look alike to the amateur eye, but in fact there are more than 240 different types of dandelions.

Dandelions, hawkweeds and hawk's-beards are familiar wild flowers of roadsides, grasslands, marshes, woodlands and uplands. Although unpopular with gardeners when they grow in lawns, they often provide the only splash of colour in urban areas and along dreary embankments.

The golden flowers and downy seed heads may seem all the same, but closer study shows a multitude of different types of dandelion, often restricted to a particular soil type or habitat. The common dandelion (*Taraxacum officinale*) was once regarded as a single species, with other dandelions classified separately. Today, however, all dandelions are regarded as *Taraxacum officinale*. The species is subdivided into about 240–250 different 'microspecies', such as the marsh dandelion and lesser dandelion, which are grouped into nine sections. Some of these microspecies are common, others rare, and most are very difficult for a non-expert to tell apart.

Hawkweed and hawk's-beard, close relatives of the dandelion, are also restricted by habitat – some are found only in uplands and others are restricted to lowland areas or marshes. A few are very scarce in Britain, found in just one or two sites, while a number of others have been introduced, often by accident, and have become well established in some places.

Flowers and clocks
Dandelions and their relatives are members of the family Asteraceae, which also includes daisies, thistles, ragworts and marigolds. Their flowers, which may be solitary or borne on a branched stalk,

are complex, composed of tiny individual florets that form a compact head and look like a single flower. Protective bracts form a collar-like or cup-like structure around the flower head. These are green and leaf-like, unlike the scaly brown bracts of most plants.

The flower heads of dandelions and their relatives are composed entirely of ray-florets – minute flowers with petals fused into a tube that opens out at the end. They are almost always yellow. Other members of the Asteraceae have a central disk of shorter florets, called disk-florets.

The other striking feature of these flowers is the seed head. The numerous individual fruits are stalked, each ending in a white, feathery device called a pappus, which floats away on the wind. In this way, the plants rapidly colonise new habitats. The seed head may be in the well-known form of a 'clock', or, in the case of hawkweeds and hawk's-beards, a dense tuft of white down.

Culinary uses
Both tea and coffee can be made from dandelions and the leaves were once favoured as a salad vegetable. They are

A field full of dandelions is a heartening sight. From March through to October these robust plants create an explosion of sunshine yellow wherever they are left to grow unhindered.

still eaten, especially in France, where they are known for their diuretic effect. It is best to avoid wild plants that have not been grown specially for consumption because they may be contaminated. When dandelion stems and leaves are damaged, they exude a milky sap that may stain human skin. The sap probably deters grazing slugs and snails.

DANDELION FACT FILE

● **Dandelion**
Taraxacum officinale
(section *Ruderalia*)
Habitat and distribution
Common and widespread in grassy habitats, including lawns, verges, meadows and wasteland; up to about 1500m (5000ft)
Size Up to 35cm (14in) tall
Key features
Hairless perennial; deeply toothed leaves in compact basal rosette; hollow flower stalks rise from centre; flower heads bright yellow, solitary, 25–75mm (1–3in) across, often with down-turned bracts; fruits long-stalked, usually grey-brown, with feathery pappus, forming spherical 'clock'
Flowering time
All year, but mainly March–October

● **Lesser dandelion**
Taraxacum officinale
(section *Erythrosperma*)
Habitat and distribution
Widespread on warm, dry grasslands, dunes, chalk downs, cliff tops and rocky habitats; in most of Britain apart from parts of central Wales, north-west England, most of western and central Scotland; in Ireland mainly coastal
Size Up to 30cm (12in) tall
Key features
Hairless perennial; deeply toothed leaves in basal rosette, narrower and shorter than common dandelion and solitary flower heads smaller, 15–30mm (⅝–1¼in) across, often pale yellow; fruits often purplish red
Flowering time
April–June

● **Red-veined dandelion**
Taraxacum officinale
(section *Spectabilia*)
Habitat and distribution
Damp grassy places, often in mountain pastures and on ledges
Size Up to 40cm (16in) tall
Key features
Hairless perennial; sharply lobed or unlobed leaves often with reddish stalk and midrib, sometimes several red spots; solitary flower heads 35–55mm (1⅜–2¼in) across; bracts broad, with no backward curves; outer florets reddish below
Flowering time
June–July

● **Narrow-leaved marsh dandelion**
Taraxacum officinale
(section *Palustria*)
Habitat and distribution
Open grassy places in marshes, fens and riversides, usually at low altitude
Size Up to 35cm (14in) tall
Key features
Hairless perennial; leaves very narrow and finely toothed, occasionally untoothed; flower heads 25–40mm (1–1½in) across; bracts tightly pressed against flower stalk, broad with pale margin
Flowering time
June–early July

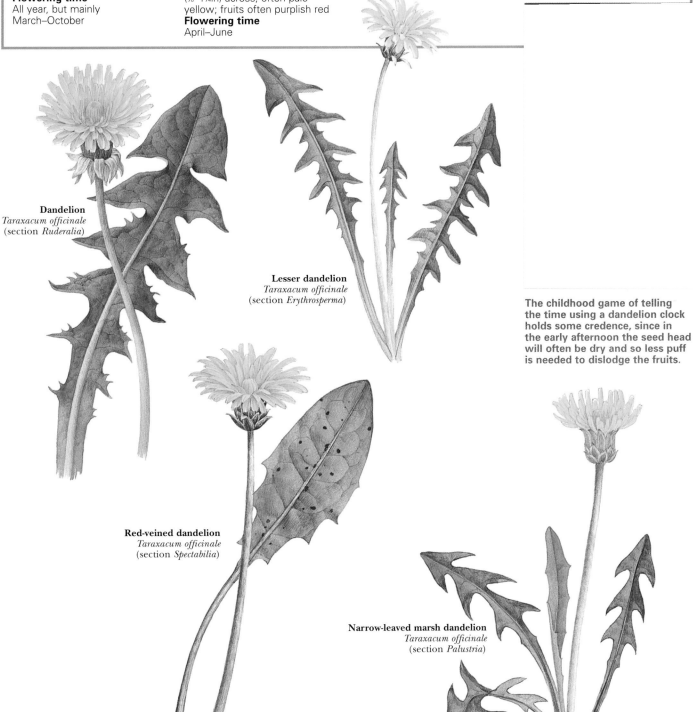

Dandelion
Taraxacum officinale
(section *Ruderalia*)

Lesser dandelion
Taraxacum officinale
(section *Erythrosperma*)

Red-veined dandelion
Taraxacum officinale
(section *Spectabilia*)

Narrow-leaved marsh dandelion
Taraxacum officinale
(section *Palustria*)

The childhood game of telling the time using a dandelion clock holds some credence, since in the early afternoon the seed head will often be dry and so less puff is needed to dislodge the fruits.

HAWK'S-BEARD FACT FILE

● Smooth hawk's-beard
Crepis capillaris
Habitat and distribution
Widespread and common in grasslands, roadsides, heaths and dry, disturbed ground, usually at low altitudes
Size Up to 75cm (30in) tall
Key features
Annual or biennial; sometimes with sticky hairs but often hairless; flower heads smaller than those of other species, 10–15mm (⅜–⅝in) across, outer florets reddish beneath; bracts sepal-like, partially spreading; leaves deeply lobed, shiny, most forming basal rosette, a few higher on stem
Flowering time
June–December

● Stinking hawk's-beard
Crepis foetida
Habitat and distribution
Very rare, declared extinct in 1980 but reintroduced to coastal shingle in Kent
Size Up to 50cm (20in) tall
Key features
Annual or biennial; flower heads borne on drooping stems when in bud, more erect when open, 15–20mm (⅝–¾in) across; basal leaves with large diamond-shaped end lobe, densely hairy; scent reminiscent of bitter almonds when crushed
Flowering time
June–August

● Marsh hawk's-beard
Crepis paludosa
Habitat and distribution
Widespread in northern Britain and Ireland in marshes, wet meadows, streamsides and wet woodlands, mainly on hills
Size Up to 90cm (36in) tall
Key features
Almost hairless perennial; flowers orange-yellow, heads 15–25mm (⅝–1in) across; bracts sepal-like, downy with sticky, blackish hairs; lance-shaped, sharply toothed leaves clasp stem
Flowering time
June–September

● Northern hawk's-beard or soft hawk's-beard
Crepis mollis
Habitat and distribution
Scarce and decreasing in woods, streamsides and fens on mineral-rich soils in parts of northern England and north-east Scotland
Size Up to 60cm (24in) or so tall
Key features
Slender, hairy or sometimes hairless perennial; leaves not, or only sparsely, toothed, with rounded bases clasping stem; flower heads large, 20–30mm (¾–1¼in) across, in loose cluster; pappus pure white
Flowering time
July–August

● Beaked hawk's-beard
Crepis vesicaria
Habitat and distribution
Widespread and spreading in southern Britain and Ireland on roadsides, waste ground, embankments, rough fields, usually on calcareous, or chalky, soils; introduced from eastern Europe in 1713
Size Up to 80cm (32in) tall
Key features
Slightly downy perennial; leaves sharply lobed, half-clasping the often reddish stem; flower heads yellow, 15–25mm (⅝–1in) across, in loose, branched clusters, upright in bud; outer florets usually reddish; fruits with long beaks
Flowering time
May–July

● Bristly hawk's-beard
Crepis setosa
Habitat and distribution
Introduced from southern and central Europe; scarce on disturbed ground, refuse tips, rough grassland and roadsides
Size Up to 30cm (12in) tall
Key features
Bristly biennial; flowers pale yellow, 15–25mm (⅝–1in) across; outer bracts short and spreading; upper stem bristly; dandelion-like leaves deeply lobed, clasping stem
Flowering time
July–September

● Rough hawk's-beard
Crepis biennis
Habitat and distribution
Scattered throughout England, mainly in south-east, and Ireland, mainly in east; in grassy places, farmland and waste ground, especially on calcareous soils; becoming scarce
Size Up to 120cm (48in) tall
Key features
Taller than other hawk's-beards, with fewer flowers; biennial; flower heads large, rich yellow, 20–35mm (¾–1⅜in) across, outer florets yellow beneath; large, stalked, dandelion-like leaves, half-clasping often reddish stem
Flowering time
June–July

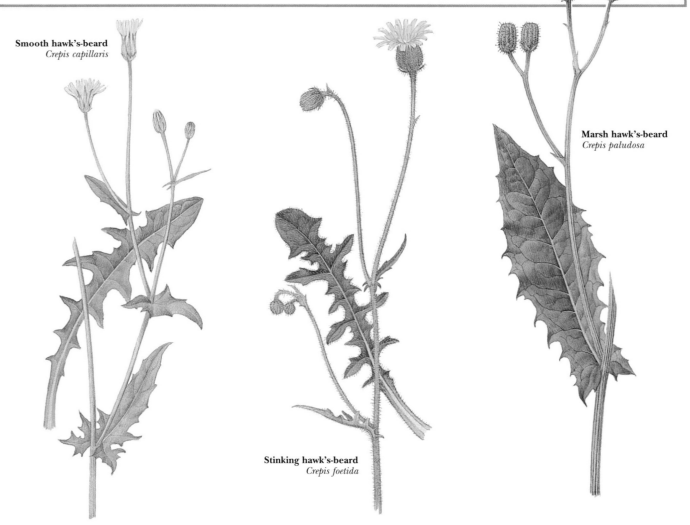

Smooth hawk's-beard
Crepis capillaris

Stinking hawk's-beard
Crepis foetida

Marsh hawk's-beard
Crepis paludosa

Bristly hawk's-beard
Crepis setosa

Each flower head is made up of
hundreds of ray-florets, each with a
single, elongated petal tube that
flattens out at its outer end.

Beaked hawk's-beard
Crepis vesicaria

Rough hawk's-beard
Crepis biennis

**Northern hawk's-beard or
soft hawk's-beard**
Crepis mollis

Because of the long
flowering period enjoyed
by many of these species,
flowers and seed heads can
often be seen alongside
each other.

HAWKWEED FACT FILE

● **Mouse-ear hawkweed**
Pilosella officinarum
Habitat and distribution
Widespread and common in most of Britain on bare, dry grassy places on a range of soil types
Size Up to 30cm (12in) tall
Key features
Hairy perennial with greyish, slightly inrolled, untoothed leaves; flowers lemon yellow, solitary, heads up to 30mm (1¼in) across; outer florets usually reddish beneath; runners growing from basal rosette bear small leaves that are spaced out
Flowering time
May–October

● **Alpine hawkweed**
Hieracium holosericeum
Habitat and distribution
Grassy ledges, rocky places in Scottish Highlands only
Size Up to 20cm (8in) tall
Key features
Hairy perennial with basal rosette of untoothed, greyish leaves with winged stalks; flower stalk very hairy, sometimes with small clasping bract-like leaves; flower solitary, 25–35mm (1–1⅜in) across
Flowering time
July–August

● **Narrow-leaved hawkweed**
Hieracium umbellatum
Habitat and distribution
Widespread and common in dry grassy and heathy places, usually on slightly acidic soils
Size Up to 80cm (32in) tall
Key features
Softly hairy perennial with narrow, slightly toothed stem leaves, lacks basal rosette; flowers yellow, 20–30mm (¾–1¼in) across, in loose clusters on erect stalks; pappus form loose head
Flowering time
June–November

There are a large number of very similar hawkweed microspecies in Britain – about 260 divided into 15 sections. While these do exhibit subtle differences in the form and arrangement of leaves and flower heads, their distributions and habitat preferences are usually the best clues to identification.

● *Hieracium lingulatum* is found only in the mountains of Scotland, growing on streamsides and rocky ledges above about 450m (1500ft)

● *Hieracium anglicum* is widespread in mountainous regions of Britain, usually on rocky ledges and streamsides on mineral-rich and calcareous rocks.

● *Hieracium dewarii* is found mainly on rocky streamsides in central and western Scotland.

● *Hieracium prenanthoides*, is common on some grassy banks and ledges in parts of Wales, northern England and Scotland.

● *Hieracium sabaudum* is common on heaths and sandy soils in open woodlands in mainland Britain and south-east Ireland.

● *Hieracium trichocaulon* is widespread and common in southern and eastern England, rarer elsewhere, on sandy heaths and woodland tracks.

● *Hieracium latobrigorum* is common in Scotland, but scarce or absent elsewhere, occurring in rocky and grassy places in hilly areas, but never at high altitude.

● *Hieracium britannicum* is restricted to the carboniferous limestone of the Peak District and surrounding areas, where it is relatively common.

● *Hieracium decolor* is common on carboniferous limestone in northern England.

● *Hieracium orcadense* is scattered across western and northern Britain, including Orkney, in coastal and upland grasslands, and in rocky areas on calcareous soils.

● *Hieracium vulgatum* is the most common hawkweed in northern Britain, in grassy and rocky areas.

● *Hieracium acuminatum* is common in lowland areas in England on roadsides, grassy areas and rough ground but scarcer in the north of Britain.

● *Hieracium caledonicum* is widespread on limestone in northern England, Scotland, northern Wales and northern Ireland.

Mouse-ear hawkweed
Pilosella officinarum

Narrow-leaved hawkweed
Hieracium umbellatum

Alpine hawkweed
Hieracium holosericeum

WILDLIFE WATCH

Where do dandelions grow?

● Once, dandelions and hawkweeds could be found on farmland anywhere in Britain. Now they have been banished from most farms by regular use of herbicides. They still occur on roadsides, waste ground, gardens and old, undisturbed pastures, quickly colonising newly disturbed ground.

● Mountain ledges, streamsides and cliff tops where grazing pressure is absent are ideal places to search for alpine hawkweeds and hawk's-beards. Most of these species flower late in the summer.

● Fens and marshes, especially those with a network of drainage channels and raised banks, are good sites for damp habitat species such as narrow-leaved marsh dandelion and marsh hawk's-beard.

● Heathlands, sandy woodland rides, sand dunes and heavily grazed downland are the places to look for the lesser dandelion and mouse-ear hawkweed.

Woodland watch

- The badger
- The family life of foxes
- The great spotted woodpecker
- Recognising finches
- Centipedes and millipedes
- Orange-tip butterfly
- Anemones and relatives
- Wild violets

The badger

Superbly adapted to their subterranean lifestyle, these instantly recognisable animals were once in sharp decline. Now that they are fully protected by the law, their numbers are increasing every year.

Until a few decades ago, little was known about the habits of badgers – although large and distinctive, they were considered reclusive creatures of the night, unlikely to be encountered up close. But badgers had good reason to be shy of human contact. In addition to generations of persecution by gamekeepers, their setts, as their burrow systems are called, were regularly disrupted by badger baiters seeking to pit fierce dogs against them – an illegal activity then, as now.

Fortunately, things are very different today. The badger has a large number of ardent supporters, with more than 80 badger groups around the country working to monitor their local populations and observe them in their natural environment. Much of this change came about through the books of the late Dr Ernest Neal. An English schoolmaster and naturalist, Dr Neal described how anyone could enjoy the thrill of watching badgers in the wild, with no special equipment beyond a torch and perhaps some insect repellent. Thanks to his work in educating the public, and more enlightened attitudes to wildlife in general, badgers now have

Scraping tree trunks or stumps helps to clean the badger's long claws. It may also be a form of territorial marking, leaving scent, as well as scratches, on the wood as a message to other badgers.

CURIOUS STRIPES

The badger is grizzled grey on its back, with a black underside and legs. The face is white with a broad black stripe up each side over the eye – but why? Badgers are not only nocturnal but also subterranean, so what purpose can a striped face serve? Why are they not black, or grey, all over?

Some have suggested these markings actually make the animal harder to see in the dappled shadows caused by moonlight filtering through the trees.

Another, less plausible, suggestion is that the striped face may be easier to see underground, allowing badgers to recognise each other. The problem with this idea is that total darkness reigns underground at night and nothing can be seen at all. Moreover, badgers are known to recognise other individuals by scent, not by sight.

It has also been suggested that the black and white stripes serve as a warning, but to whom? Badgers do not have any significant natural predators. Few other animals would attempt to tackle such a large creature, especially one armed with such long claws and powerful jaws.

No one seems to know.

BADGER FACT FILE

The badger is about the size of a smallish dog, with an unmistakable stripy face and tapering snout. It has a thick-set, wedge-shaped body, short legs and a shaggy white-tipped tail. Badgers normally live in or near woodland, spending much time underground.

● NAMES
Common name: badger
Scientific name: *Meles meles*

● HABITAT
Farmland, woodlands, even suburban areas, especially where there is cover among shrubs and access to good feeding areas; grasslands and cereal fields; prefers areas of well-drained soil in which to burrow, especially on slopes

● DISTRIBUTION
Throughout mainland Britain and Ireland, except in parts of northern Scotland; scarce in lowland areas of Lancashire and East Anglia, absent from Isle of Man and most Scottish islands, but present on the Isle of Wight and Anglesey

● STATUS
Currently estimated at just over 300,000 individuals in Britain

● SIZE
Length 68–80cm (27–32in), tail 15cm (6in), ear 3cm (1¼in); weight 8–14kg (18–31lb). Females generally about 10% smaller

● FEATURES
Shaggy, coarse grey fur, striped face and black belly

● HABITS
Nocturnal; occupies clan territories within which members of other social groups are unwelcome; often inactive for long periods in winter, but do not hibernate

● FOOD
Earthworms, beetles, wasps and other insects, small mammals, birds' eggs, roots, fruits, cereal crops and a wide range of other food

● BREEDING
1–5 cubs born January–April, peaking in February. Cubs emerge above ground at about 8 weeks old

● YOUNG
Similar to adults but smaller, with a shorter snout

● SIGNS
Droppings often soft and deposited in small pits; distinctive hairs caught on fence wires; characteristic footprints in mud; setts with many large entrances, 20–30cm (8–12in) or more in diameter

Badgers are fully protected by the Badgers Act of 1973 plus the Wildlife and Countryside Act 1981. Separate legislation passed in 1985 protects setts. It is illegal to catch badgers, kill them, allow dogs to worry them, keep them as pets or obstruct their burrows.

Distribution map key

■ Present all year round

□ Not present

The most distinctive feature of the badger is its black-and-white striped face. The reason for these markings is unknown.

Very coarse and somewhat crinkly hairs have a white tip above a black band and a yellowish white base.

The tail often has brown discoloration around the base, caused by secretions from hidden scent glands.

COSY BEDDING

It is cool underground and possibly damp as well, so in order to make the sett more comfortable badgers bring in large amounts of bedding in the form of dry grass, bracken or other suitable dry vegetation. They rake up the grass using their front paws, tuck a bundle between their forearms and chin and shuffle backwards to the sett, dragging it underground. The untidy trail left by this activity is a clue to the location of a badger sett.

Badgers are scrupulously clean animals and always leave the sett to use a special toilet area outside, rather than fouling their nests. Nevertheless, the bedding gets soggy after a few months and badgers usually clean it out at the end of winter, leaving a large heap outside the sett. Among the old grass and soil, a lot of crinkly black and white hairs are an obvious sign that badgers are in residence.

A badger's front feet are powerful digging implements that can rapidly move large quantities of earth. The claws cannot be retracted and they make dangerous weapons with which the animal can defend itself if necessary.

comprehensive legal protection, which also extends to their setts. This is one reason why badger numbers have steadily increased and continue to do so.

In some areas, there may be up to 10 badgers per square kilometre (26 per square mile) and more in parts of south-west England. The reason for such success is not certain, but moist climate and plentiful pastureland, and therefore earthworms – part of their staple diet – may be important factors. Badgers are quite rare in upland areas, where the soil is often waterlogged or rocky below the surface. They are also relatively scarce in East Anglia – perhaps not fully recovered from the persecution they once suffered there.

Earth movers

With powerful limbs and big claws, badgers are great diggers, and they excavate extensive burrows in soft, sandy soils. The sett may comprise hundreds of metres (yards) of tunnels, dug out by successive generations of badgers.

Each paw is armed with long curved claws on all five toes, and the bones of the shoulder and forelimbs are modified to make best use of the powerful arm muscles, providing leverage for shifting stones and earth. Digging is done with the broad forepaws – loose earth is scooped backwards under the belly, and kicked away with the smaller hind feet.

The badger's fur is coarse and wiry with widely spaced hairs. Each hair is about 5–7cm (2–3in) long, white tipped and

Badgers generally emerge from underground about half an hour after sunset, or later in disturbed places. Winter emergence times are more erratic and in bad weather they may not come out at all.

BADGERS AND TB

The rise in badger numbers has unfortunately brought them into conflict with farmers, who accuse them of infecting cattle with bovine tuberculosis. The badger is legally protected, but some farmers want the authority to control them by culling, and this has generated a simmering controversy to rival the debate over foxhunting.

Badgers can certainly contract bovine tuberculosis (TB) in laboratory experiments and in the wild – the first badger TB victim was discovered in 1971. Farmers claim that they spread the disease among cattle by physical contact and in urine on pastures. They say there is a link between the badger population boom of the past few decades and the rise in TB in their herds. However, conservationists argue that these claims ignore everything that is known about badger habits – they usually steer well clear of larger animals – and point out that the rise in TB also coincided with increasing industrialisation of farming. They say that TB outbreaks in previously clean herds are far more likely to originate from new cattle shipped in over long distances than from distinctly stay-at-home badgers.

Successive governments have conducted studies into the problem, but with badger population and distribution still little understood, they have had difficulty coming up with any definite conclusions.

rather crinkly. Hairs caught on barbed-wire fences as the badger squeezes underneath are easy to identify. Unlike the majority of mammals, badgers lack dense, fine underfur. A coarse coat is better suited to life underground – it protects the skin from damage, but does not become clogged with soil and mud and is easily cleaned with some vigorous scratching. When badgers venture above ground each evening, they spend a lot of time grooming the soil out of their coats.

The wiry fur does not provide much insulation, but the large amount of fat accumulated beneath the skin does the

▲ These badgers are grooming each other, a behaviour that serves not only to strengthen the bond between them, but also to spread scent from one to the other, thereby ensuring that members of a social group can all recognise each other by smell.

◄ Viewed head-on, the badger's facial pattern is unmistakable. The eyes are relatively small and so are the white-tipped ears. Long whiskers protrude from either side of the mouth and nose.

same job and helps to keep them warm. This fat is also useful as a food reserve. Badgers were once thought to hibernate through winter food shortages, but it is now known that they are not true hibernators. However, they do remain inactive underground during long periods of inclement weather, relying on their fat reserves to tide them over until conditions improve.

A visit to a sett after a snowfall will usually show footprints in the snow, confirming that the badgers are still awake. This is the ideal time to note a curiosity in their tracks – because the hind feet are smaller than the front feet, footprints from a single animal can often look like two animals of different sizes walking in single file.

Varied diet

Badgers emerge from the sett each evening at dusk, about the time the last birds stop singing, and after grooming, they set off to feed, usually alone. They rely mainly on smell to find their way about and locate good feeding places – badgers' eyesight is fairly poor and cubs are especially short-sighted. Usually, they trot or amble around with a rolling gait, slowing to sniff around carefully in promising areas for food. If alarmed, badgers can show a surprising burst of speed, sprinting off at up to 30 kilometres per hour (18mph) over short distances. They can also climb, using their claws and powerful forelimbs to grip rough stonework or the bark of logs. Sloping trees are often explored and badger hairs may be found more than three metres (10ft) above the ground.

Badgers belong to the same family as weasels and stoats, the Mustelidae, which also includes otters, mink and polecats. These are all predatory animals and, like their relatives, badgers eat small mammals and frogs, and will relish a nest full of

A POWERFUL BITE

Badgers have a basically carnivorous dentition, but the molar teeth are broad and knobbly for grinding up tough nuts and gritty worms. The jaws have such a strong hinge that they cannot be detached, even in a clean skull, that is one from which all hair and flesh have been removed – no other British mammal has such firmly attached jaws. The skull has a high crest along its ridge to provide increased area for the attachment of enlarged jaw muscles.

All this enables the badger to deliver the most powerful bite of any British mammal, said to be strong enough to leave dents in a metal spade.

The badger's mighty bite is used in defence, for tearing up tough, meaty prey and also to break up wood when looking for insect grubs that live inside tree stumps.

baby rabbits or birds' eggs. They will kill and eat hedgehogs too – their long claws and strong forelimbs enable them to prise open even a tightly rolled hedgehog, an impossible task for most other predators. Hedgehogs are rarely found in large populations when many badgers are present and, in some areas, badgers can be a significant threat to the continued survival of the local hedgehog population.

The badger does, however, have a wide-ranging diet and also eats a lot of smaller creatures. For instance, badgers will eagerly dig out wasp nests or nests of solitary bees to feast on their larvae and any stores of honey that might be present, their long coarse fur protecting them from retaliatory stings. Invertebrates such as earthworms and beetles are nutritious, yet do not require much effort to catch.

Earthworms in particular play an important part in the badger's diet, although their contribution varies from place to place. The availability of worms may be one of the factors that limits badger numbers in certain parts of the country, and may also affect population density and social group structure. In dry weather, worms stay deep and inactive in the soil, so long periods of drought can cause serious problems for badgers, especially cubs – many will die in a long, hot summer. It is likely that Britain's warm, wet summers, especially in the south-west, have helped badgers reach their present high numbers, but a few long dry summers could still result in a significant population crash.

Badgers sometimes feed as a group when a concentration of tasty food is found outside the sett. This may include peanuts or raisins, scattered there by hopeful badger watchers.

Although carnivorous, badgers will supplement their diet with vegetable matter, including bluebell bulbs, wild arum corms and, in rural areas, even garden bulbs in the spring. Fruits, such as blackberries and bilberries in upland areas and fallen apples in orchards and gardens, are a favourite in the autumn. Beech mast (the fruit of beech trees) and acorns are also relished.

Their plant-eating habits can lead badgers into raiding cereal crops, where they not only consume the grain, but also roll in the ripening corn, making it difficult to harvest properly. They are particularly fond of maize and the increasing prevalence of this crop in modern farming is another probable factor in the badger's rising numbers.

Raising young

Badgers do not normally breed until they are at least two years old, although earlier breeding is not unknown. They mate during spring, but the development of the embryos is delayed for many weeks before normal pregnancy starts. The cubs – up to five – may be born any time from January to April but mostly they arrive in February, which ensures that when they leave the sett eight weeks later, food is plentiful.

At first, the cubs have pink skin covered with a thin layer of silky white fur, and the facial stripes are barely visible. The milk

Young badgers have little to fear from predators – dogs may kill a few, foxes may occasionally snatch a very young unprotected cub and adult badgers have been known to kill them occasionally. Nevertheless, about 50 per cent of cubs do not survive to one year old.

Annual road deaths may be as high as 10,000, and inexperienced cubs are particularly at risk of being run over, as are young badgers in areas of high population density, as they roam in search of new feeding places.

▼ Badgers tend to use the same routes on their nightly forays. Generation after generation of young badgers will follow well-worn paths through the vegetation, passing across fields and under fences, on foraging expeditions.

▲ Cubs spend several weeks underground before they first emerge in spring Their characteristic short, blunt muzzles elongate with age until, at about eight months old, their faces resemble those of their parents.

▲ It is not unknown for badgers to drink in hot weather, although their food normally contains enough moisture. Look for their distinctive footprints in the mud near water, particularly ditches where crossing points have been identified.

teeth do not appear for a month or so, and the cubs spend their first eight weeks underground, slowly growing into miniature versions of their parents.

When the nights at last start to get warmer, the young make their first appearance above ground. They still depend on their mother for milk at this stage and are not weaned until about 12 weeks old. If food is scarce, they can take milk for much longer, and may not be fully weaned for four to six months. However, normally they grow quickly, especially if there are plenty of worms available, and can weigh as much as 10kg (22lb) by the end of their first year.

Youthful high spirits

Play among young badger cubs probably helps to cement the bonds within the social group. This becomes important as they grow older, when they will spread out to forage alone each night before returning to the sett.

These young badgers are discovering the delights of playing on a low tree branch. They duck under and swing from it while hanging from their front paws. They also scratch deeply into the wood.

Badgers relish mock fights and other energetic play when free of the confines of their sett.

The family life of foxes

Four-week-old cubs emerge from their den in spring and spend the next few months of their lives learning, through play, the skills and legendary cunning that will help them survive as adults.

Among the most successful of British mammals, the fox is an adaptable creature. Its natural home is the woods, but it can thrive in many different environments ranging from city streets to mountains. Foxes have adapted to encroaching towns and cities by learning to take advantage of humans, rather than retreating into the dwindling pockets of unspoilt countryside. Resourceful and bold, their reputation for cunning is well deserved.

Throughout their first spring and summer, as they grow to adolescence, young foxes are at their most charming and boisterous and, with their spread to urban areas, the enchanting sight of a fox family at play is not as unusual as it used to be.

The cubs establish strong bonds as they mature. Even when the time comes to leave their mother, they may stick together for quite a while, sharing a territory and hunting cooperatively.

Finding a den

Foxes breed just once a year and the cubs are generally born in the second half of March, or slightly later in northern Britain. A few days before giving birth, the female, or vixen, selects a suitable den for her imminent family. Although for the rest of the year they live out in the open, foxes prefer to give birth and raise their families underground.

If forced to, the vixen will dig a completely new burrow, two or three metres (6–10ft) long, but she will often enlarge part of an existing rabbit warren or move into a deserted badger sett. Sometimes a cavity among tree roots will be extended and refurbished to form a den. In mountainous areas, she may choose a deep crevice among rocks, and elsewhere a hollow tree stump or farm outbuilding may be suitable. Occasionally, the cubs will be born in dens among logs or old machinery, even amid the rusting wrecks of a car breaker's yard.

In urban areas, vixens often take up residence in buildings, even inhabited ones. Usually they shelter under the floorboards, but they may venture upstairs to the attic. The wily intruder may enter a house through the cat flap and give birth to her cubs inside, where they are safe and warm – especially in buildings that are centrally heated.

If the cubs are born in an occupied house, they can make a nuisance of themselves as they grow, chasing each other about below the floor and making a lot of noise after dark. They may also chew vital wires and pipes, and have even been known to pop up in living rooms at odd times. The most common suburban den sites, however, are in spaces underneath garden sheds. These are chosen by about 40 per cent of urban vixens as their ideal home.

Foxes do not line their dens with soft, comfortable materials, perhaps because these would present a risk of disease if

STARTING OUT

At the age of about four weeks – usually in April or early May – fox cubs begin to moult. They lose their brown baby fur and start to grow a new coat that will be similar in colour to an adult's coat. This develops first on the face, which also changes shape. The ears of young foxes become larger and more pointed, and their muzzles lengthen to form the typical pointed snout. By mid-May, most cubs are about six weeks old, and look more like miniature versions of their parents. At this time, they begin to make their first wary excursions away from the den.

A SNUG DEN

Outside the breeding season, foxes rarely use burrows, preferring to brave the elements above ground. When it is time to give birth, however, a den is an important asset. The vixen excavates a new burrow or enlarges an existing one, or she may create a chamber in a surprisingly small cavity among the roots of a tree or in a rocky crevice. Even a pregnant vixen can squeeze through a gap less than 15cm (6in) in diameter to gain access. The young family must be protected from the weather and kept safe from humans and dogs.

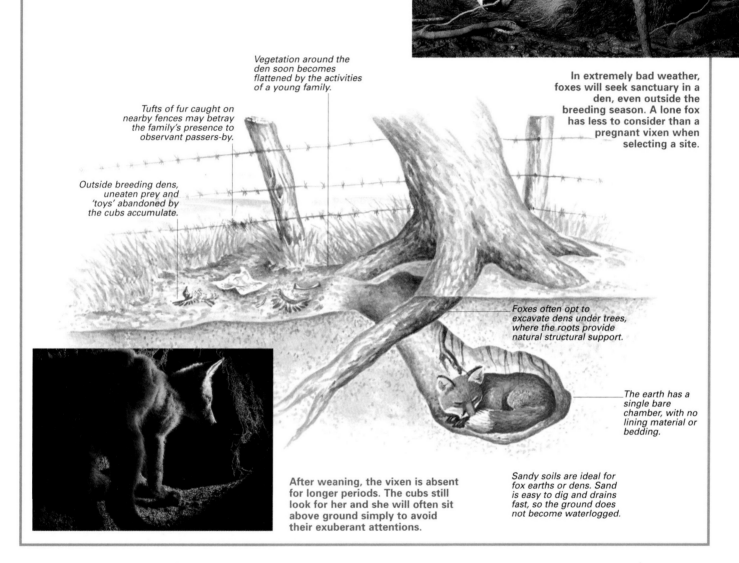

Tufts of fur caught on nearby fences may betray the family's presence to observant passers-by.

Vegetation around the den soon becomes flattened by the activities of a young family.

Outside breeding dens, uneaten prey and 'toys' abandoned by the cubs accumulate.

In extremely bad weather, foxes will seek sanctuary in a den, even outside the breeding season. A lone fox has less to consider than a pregnant vixen when selecting a site.

Foxes often opt to excavate dens under trees, where the roots provide natural structural support.

The earth has a single bare chamber, with no lining material or bedding.

After weaning, the vixen is absent for longer periods. The cubs still look for her and she will often sit above ground simply to avoid their exuberant attentions.

Sandy soils are ideal for fox earths or dens. Sand is easy to dig and drains fast, so the ground does not become waterlogged.

they became soiled. However, since a bare hole is not very cosy, the vixen remains with her family constantly for the first two weeks to keep them warm, only leaving the den briefly to relieve herself. The dog (male) fox is excluded from the den while the cubs are being born, but he later plays a valuable role, fetching food for the vixen and their growing family.

Where fox numbers are low, a fox family may consist of just the dog and vixen, who will raise four or five cubs. Where numbers are higher, some subordinate adults do not breed but act as aunts or uncles, collecting food and helping to raise a parent's, offspring's or sibling's family instead. Occasionally, two closely related foxes share the same den, creating a larger family than usual. Recent

genetic research has shown that subordinate females quite often produce young themselves and litters may be mixed together. At other times, however, the young of subordinate females are killed – it is not clear which fox kills them or why. Having additional pregnant females in the group does mean that there is a 'standby' litter if something happens to the main breeding female, but killing the extra cubs at birth could save the group from rearing too many offspring for the food resources available.

Very young fox cubs bear little resemblance to their parents, having dark chocolate-brown velvety fur with short muzzles, snub noses and rounded faces. The red coat starts to appear after about a month.

First weeks

At birth, fox cubs are blind and deaf, weigh about 100g (3½oz) each, and are some 10cm (4in) long. For their first few days, they lie close alongside the vixen, feeding regularly and growing quite slowly. Their eyes open in the second week and after this the cubs become more active, crawling around rather unsteadily. In a small den this is not a problem, but where the vixen has made a larger space, under a garden shed for instance, she may have to get up and retrieve the cubs repeatedly as they wander off in all directions. If they stray too far, the cubs will utter a weak triple bark, a signal for their mother to come and fetch them. Secure with their mother underground, the cubs are generally safe from danger. However, in very wet weather the den may become damp and cold, or perhaps a badger will find the young cubs and kill them. Despite all the care the vixen takes to ensure the safety of her young family, about 15 per cent of baby foxes never see the outside world – they die before they get the chance to emerge above ground.

Above ground

However, the majority of cubs survive to a few weeks old at least and it is soon time for them to emerge above ground. If the spring weather is fine, the cubs frolic around the entrance to the den, endlessly chasing each other and engaging in playful fights.

Their games create a large open space in front of the den where the surrounding grass and vegetation is flattened. In gardens, plant pots, garden labels and ornaments or other delicate items that get in the way will be playfully vandalised, as the cubs chew them or engage in tug-of-war games. In the countryside, sticks and the odd rabbit bone all serve as pretend prey to be dragged about, tossed in the air and pounced on as they fall. While the cubs

FEEDING VIXEN

When the cubs are born, the vixen loses all the fur on her belly, making it easier for them to suckle. There are eight teats, plenty to go round for the average family of four or five babies, and the cubs rely on her exclusively for the first month of their lives.

At first, the vixen lies down while her family feeds. However, as the cubs get older and bigger, there is not enough room for them all to suckle properly, so she stands up to allow them all to feed. Her supply of milk gradually begins to dry up, so that by the time the cubs are six weeks old they will be forced to rely increasingly on solid food. Even so, whenever the vixen returns to her young cubs, she is greeted enthusiastically. Although they are eating some solid food, the cubs are still keen for a feed of milk. On this fatty diet, they put on 50 grams (1¾oz) a day until they are 10 weeks old.

Cubs continue to suckle until they are at least six weeks old. The growing young jostle for position as the vixen patiently stands and endures their sharp teeth.

▲ The vixen relies on her mate to bring food to keep her strong. Later on, when the cubs are weaned, the male must bring enough rats, voles, rabbits, birds and scraps to feed the whole family.

► With most of the meat gone, a moorhen carcass still provides a cub with the opportunity to strengthen his teeth and jaws, crunching the bones up small.

undoubtedly enjoy these games, they also serve to develop the young foxes' skills, strength and coordination. They need constant practice if they are to become good hunters and killers – a clumsy or inefficient fox will not survive for long once the family breaks up.

Weaning starts when the cubs are about one month old and they begin to grow their adult coat and look more like their parents. If the parents catch small prey – voles and birds, for instance – at some distance from the den, they swallow it and regurgitate it later for the cubs to eat. Larger items, such as dead rabbits or meat bones stolen from dog bowls or found lying in gardens, may be carefully carried back to the den.

The cubs will spend hours gnawing at bones and squabbling for possession of scraps, as play and feeding blend together. The bones are a valuable source of calcium, essential for the cub's growth. Gnawing at them also strengthens developing jaws and teeth. As with most mammals, the cubs' first teeth do not last for long – just like human milk teeth, they fall out and are replaced by permanent adult dentition as the animal matures.

A lot of the food brought to the den is accompanied by inedible debris such as fur, feathers, fish-and-chip wrappers and

fried-chicken boxes, which accumulates as untidy evidence of the fox family's diet. It may even include an occasional hedgehog skin scavenged from a roadside corpse. Soft toys, shoes or rubber balls may also lie among the litter, brought back by the adults for the cubs to chew and play with.

Learning curve

From about May onwards, the cubs are learning where to find food and how to catch prey for themselves. On warm, damp evenings, the family may go out to search for earthworms lying on the ground among grass and leaves. These are easy prey for the cubs. They may also stumble across the occasional baby mouse or bird. The cubs are not yet as adept as the adults at capturing such active prey, so their diet tends to include more worms, fruit and insects than that of their elders.

Play is an important part of growing up. Play-fighting helps the cubs to gain strength and coordination, and to learn strategies that may one day be used in earnest in dominance battles. Cub fights are boisterous but rarely serious.

Fighting fit

The cubs spend the entire summer together as a family, sleeping in the day and emerging at night to play. Although games are fun, play-fighting also allows the cubs to establish their place in the group's hierarchy.

The cubs learn from an early age the facial expressions and postures needed to assert dominance or express submission.

The hierarchy established among siblings comes into effect when an adult returns with food. The dominant cub usually gets the meal.

Dwarfed by bluebells, the cub's light-coloured eyes take in all around it. If it wanders too far away and becomes scared, the cub calls for its mother.

As summer progresses, the family may move from an underground den to somewhere more airy and spacious, and better suited to accommodate the rapidly growing cubs. They frequently lie up in dense undergrowth, coming out on warm days to bask in the sun. As the cubs become increasingly able to fend for themselves, the older animals gradually bring less and less food, forcing the youngsters into self-sufficiency.

By September, the cubs are almost as big as their parents. Their tails begin to lose their thin and pointed shape as the young foxes develop the thick, bushy fur and round-ended tail of adults.

One third of cubs do not survive to six months old, usually the victims of accidents. Many are run over on the road, some drown in garden ponds and swimming pools, and others die entangled in garden netting or plastic litter. Sad though the sight of a young dead fox is, such losses are a vital part of regulating the population – particularly in urban areas with few other threats.

Young wanderlust

By late summer, the surviving cubs are able to look after themselves, and at this stage many of the young foxes leave their parents' territory to find their own place to live. In areas where fox densities are low, particularly out in the open countryside, in rural woodlands

As the cubs grow older, they wander off by themselves in search of beetles and worms. At this stage, the cubs are less wary than their parents and therefore easier to watch.

Early adventures

The first few excursions beyond the confines of the den are full of excitement for young fox cubs. They emerge with the onset of warmer weather in April or May, when the countryside is alive with new sounds and scents. Under the watchful gaze of their family group, the youngsters explore the nearby area and lie up in dense vegetation.

◄ Free of the restrictions of the den, the cubs enjoy rolling around. This may help to relieve itching as the dark brown fur moults and the reddish adult pelt develops.

▲ Young cubs tire quickly and spend a large part of the day sleeping. Outside, they do so under the watchful eye of their mother.

and on moors and mountains, the young foxes may travel as much as 50km (30 miles) before establishing a new territory. However, in towns and other densely populated areas there seems to be less dispersal. In fact, many young females may have their own families within a few metres (yards) of where they themselves were born.

Both parents are diligent in the care of their young. Although the male has little to do with his offspring while they are in the den, once above ground he will groom them and play rough-and-tumble games with them.

WILDLIFE WATCH

Where can I find a fox's den?

● Breeding dens may be newly excavated or simply cleaned out and refurbished, so fresh piles of soil are often apparent. Once the cubs are born, the remains of food, such as birds' wings or rabbits' feet, may build up. A smell of rotting food, with its attendant flies, may also emanate from within the den.

● If you find a den, it is very important not to disturb the family, as the vixen will move her cubs to a new location at the slightest disruption from people or dogs. Be very quiet, keep downwind of the den and do not go too close.

● For more information about foxes, contact the Mammal Society at 15 Cloisters House, 8 Battersea Park Road, London SW8 4BG. Telephone 020 7498 4358 www.mammal.org.uk

● In south-east England, especially Kent, Surrey, Sussex and south-east London, contact The Fox Project, The Old Chapel, Bradford Street, Tonbridge, Kent TN9 1AW. Telephone 01732 367397 www.innotts.co.uk/~robmel/foxproject

The great spotted woodpecker

With its unrivalled talent for excavation and elaborate courtship ritual, this handsome bird is much in evidence in the spring – listen out for the drumming sound it uses to attract a mate.

The broad and rounded wings of a great spotted woodpecker are ideal for manoeuvring when flying among tree trunks and foliage. The bird's flight is distinctly bounding and undulating.

DID YOU KNOW?
Unique adaptations of the muscles and bones in the head and neck allow the woodpecker to use its bill to drum and excavate nest holes. The bird's secret lies in the structure of the bill and the front of the skull. The shock of impact is partly absorbed by the large muscles attached to the upper jaw, and the rest is dissipated over a wide area of the skull via a special bony structure called the nasofrontal hinge.

Among the most colourful and distinctive birds to be seen in Britain's woodlands, great spotted woodpeckers are striking in more ways than one. Not only are they stunning in appearance, with bold black-and-white plumage, a contrasting crimson crown and reddish undertail, but they use their powerful beaks to send territorial signals across the forest.

In recent years, these attractive birds have become frequent visitors to rural, suburban and even town-centre gardens and parks close to their woodland haunts. At bird tables, the woodpecker usually operates a 'snatch and grab' strategy,

scooping up a peanut or other item before hastily retreating to the safety of a nearby tree to eat it in peace. Hanging wire mesh feeders provide a far better opportunity to appreciate the woodpecker's acrobatic skills because it will climb around on them for some time, identifying and extricating the tastiest morsel on offer. Once the woodpecker is satisfied with its selection, heavy blows from the beak break up the nuts with ease.

Sometimes, a woodpecker will choose a nut that is too large to swallow, but too small to warrant the effort of carrying it away. In this case, the bird may use its

beak to cut the nut into pieces. The smaller fragment is swallowed, while the larger piece is balanced on the breast feathers, ready to be picked up and worked on a few moments later. Thus the woodpecker has its own mobile platform on which to store a meal temporarily.

The great spotted woodpecker's tolerance of humans has made it the most familiar of four native British woodpecker

GREAT SPOTTED WOODPECKER FACT FILE

A sturdy, thrush-sized, strong-billed bird with bold black-and-white markings, the great spotted woodpecker is most often seen in undulating flight in mature woodland. In recent years, however, this adaptable species has become an increasingly familiar sight in suburban parks and gardens.

● NAMES
Common names: great spotted woodpecker, pied woodpecker
Scientific name: *Dendrocopos major*

● HABITAT
Open, mature deciduous woodlands in England and Wales; also in mixed woodland and conifer forests, especially in Scottish Highlands; other habitats from farmland and orchards to gardens – wherever there are mature trees for nesting

● DISTRIBUTION
Throughout most of Britain; absent from extreme north of Scotland, whole of Ireland and the Isle of Man

● STATUS
25,000–30,000 pairs. Numbers increasing in recent decades, with spread northward in Scotland

● SIZE
Length 22–23cm (9in); weight males 70–90g (2½–3oz), females 5g (¼oz) lighter

● KEY FEATURES
Bold black-and-white plumage with large white patch in wings; underparts creamy white with pinkish red undertail; male has red nape, absent in females; face white with black moustache

● HABITS
Clings vertically to trunks of trees; excavates holes to obtain wood-boring grubs; short-distance flight distinctly undulating; visits garden feeders, particularly during winter

● VOICE
Most frequently heard call a sharp, clear alarm '*tchik*'; drums from mid-January–late June by rapid pecking on a resonant dead branch; faster drumming than other woodpeckers – in bursts of up to a second, separated by intervals of several seconds

● FOOD
Mainly insects and grubs; acorns and pine seeds in winter; other birds' eggs and nestlings in spring and summer

● NEST
Hole in decaying or living tree, excavated by both sexes; entrance 5–6cm (2–2½in) diameter; inside 11–12cm (4½in) diameter, 25–35cm (10–14in) deep; nest sometimes re-used in later years

● EGGS
Smooth, glossy, white; clutch of 4–7 eggs laid from late April; incubated by both sexes for 10–13 days from laying of last egg; total incubation time 15 days

● YOUNG
Born naked; fed by both parents; fledge after 20–24 days, independent about 2–3 weeks later; fledgling has all-red crown, smaller, paler pinkish undertail area than adult, and narrower, duller black moustache

The signs of woodpecker feeding activity are easily detected. The birds drill holes into soft bark in order to extract the larvae of wood-boring beetles. These holes, usually over 3m (10ft) from the ground, are quite often lower down in spring and summer.

The face is white with a black moustache.

Strong bill is dark grey.

A large white patch on each wing is noticeable.

Bright white bars can be seen on the black flight feathers even when the woodpecker is perching.

Vent and 'trousers' are pinkish red.

Stiff tail feathers are used as a prop when the bird is climbing trees.

Distribution map key

 Present

Not present

Boring for insects

Great spotted woodpeckers are masters of the art of locating and extracting insects living within a tree. An important clue to the presence of potential food is the sound the wood makes when it is tapped. A hollow resonance is a sign that there may be an insect chamber inside and the woodpecker is perfectly adapted for drilling wood and removing prey.

Tapping repeatedly at the bark with his stout bill, this male woodpecker has located a wood wasp larva.

He swiftly and efficiently chisels out a hole, as much as 10cm (4in) deep, to expose the soft-bodied grub.

Extending his tongue almost 4cm (1½in) beyond the tip of his beak, the bird impales the prey on its special barbed tip.

Deftly pulling the defenceless larva from the neat hole, the woodpecker swallows it whole.

Moving down the tree, the woodpecker soon locates another wood wasp grub slightly lower down the trunk.

Unlike the smaller nuthatch, the woodpecker cannot 'walk' headfirst down the trunks of trees.

► Finding a food item that is not to its taste, a great spotted woodpecker simply spits out the offending morsel.

The great spotted woodpecker climbs trees in search of insects, clinging with the sharp claws on its feet and using its stiff tail feathers as a prop.

species. The others are the larger green woodpecker, the lesser spotted (smaller than the great spotted, but with similar markings) and the rarely seen wryneck, which no longer breeds in the British Isles.

Roosting and feeding habits

Outside the breeding season, the woodpecker's main priorities are finding a meal and retaining a safe place to roost. At the end of each day, the bird returns to a favoured site – perhaps a previous year's nest, or a new hole specially excavated for the purpose. Occasionally, more than one bird will roost in the same tree, but always in different holes. When the woodpecker arrives at its roost, it utters its typical '*tchik*' contact call. If two birds happen to arrive at the same time, antagonism may break out – even if they are a potential pair. However, this is usually avoided, since males go to roost as much as 30 minutes earlier than females.

The female is first to depart for a day's foraging. Before taking flight, she cautiously peers out from her hole, scanning the area for sparrowhawks or other threats. When confident that the coast is clear, she flies to a nearby tree, where the she pauses to preen before climbing higher up the trunk, uttering a contact call. Eventually, the female heads off into the woodlands to forage, at which point any male sharing the tree may emerge.

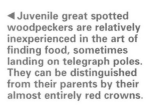

◄ Juvenile great spotted woodpeckers are relatively inexperienced in the art of finding food, sometimes landing on telegraph poles. They can be distinguished from their parents by their almost entirely red crowns.

During the winter months, woodpeckers spend most of their time searching for wood-boring beetles and their larvae in trees with dead or decaying branches, as well as in old, rotting wood. They use their beaks to hack at the bark, knocking off loose flakes with heavy blows to expose soft-bodied grubs hidden beneath.

On living trees, the bird hops about, regularly tapping the trunk with its beak. It is thought that the woodpecker listens for resonance in the wood, which may indicate the presence of a beetle or grub hidden beneath. If potential prey is detected, the bird begins to chisel out a hole up to 10cm (4in) or more deep into the trunk. When the prey is exposed, the woodpecker shoots out its tongue, which extends up to 4cm (1½in) beyond the end of the beak and has a harpoon-like tip to impale the grubs. Harder prey sticks to special bristles on the tongue that are coated with thick, sticky saliva.

Throughout the winter, tree seeds form another important part of the woodpecker's diet. This is especially true at the northern limits of the birds' distribution, in the ancient pine forests of Scotland. Pine cones removed from twigs or branches are taken to a nearby 'anvil' – a natural or specially prepared tree crevice into which the cone is wedged. The woodpecker's strong beak allows it to hammer away the scales to reach the succulent seeds within.

Drumming for a mate

Towards the end of January, great spotted woodpeckers begin to 'drum' to attract mates – the sexes maintain separate territories outside the breeding season. Drumming is at its height between March and May, and both males and females take part, striking a resonant branch about 10 to 15 times in the space of just over half a second. The woodpecker strikes its specially chosen branch so hard that the sound can be heard as far as 800 metres (half a mile) away.

The male woodpecker also performs an elaborate courtship display. When a female passes nearby, he flies across an open glade with slow, fluttering wing

◄ From mid-March, great spotted woodpeckers can be seen excavating nest holes. Both birds in a pair take turns and the hole may be completed in as little as two to three weeks.

▼ As the woodpecker chicks approach the point of fledging, conditions within the nest chamber become cramped and smelly. Despite this, the young birds finally emerge looking clean and resplendent in their black-and-white plumage.

LESSER SPOTTED WOODPECKER

No larger than a sparrow, the lesser spotted is Britain's smallest woodpecker. Secretive by nature, the bird can be hard to study, since it forages high in the tallest trees. Often only the 'pee-pee-pee-pee-pee-pee-pee-pee' song, weak 'tchik' call and drumming reveal the bird's presence. Its drumming is less frequent, softer, more rattling and longer than that of the great spotted – 'rolls' usually last for over a second without fading or a drop in pitch.

The lesser spotted lacks the large white wing patch of its larger cousin, but does have distinctive black-and-white bands across its folded wings – hence it is sometimes called the barred woodpecker. The male has a red crown, but the female lacks any red at all – the only British woodpecker except for the rare wryneck with this distinction.

It favours woodland and old hedgerows with large, mature trees, but can also be found in parkland, orchards and among riverside alders. Its range is mainly restricted to southern and western England, the Midlands and Wales. The largest populations are in the south and Midlands, but the bird could nowhere be described as common: numbers have declined by more than 75 per cent over the past 25 years, to only 3000 to 6000 pairs. This may be linked to the decline of mature elms due to Dutch elm disease.

◄ Juvenile lesser spotted woodpeckers are vulnerable when they first leave the nest. Due to their small size, they are an easy target for predators, and sit unobtrusively among the foliage for much of the time.

▶ Like its greater cousin, the lesser spotted woodpecker has broad, rounded wings that are dark but marked with white spots. Its nest hole is excavated in decaying wood, often on the underside of a branch.

beats. The pair may engage in a spiralling chase around a tree. Eventually, the male manages to persuade the female to stay in his territory in readiness for breeding.

If a suitable nest hole is not available, the woodpecker pair will now begin to excavate one – ideally in a dead or decaying tree. For the next two to four weeks, the male and female take turns at pecking out the hole. Nest and roosting holes no longer used by woodpeckers provide excellent nest sites for other species, including tits, nuthatches and especially starlings.

Egg laying begins in late April or early May and incubation starts once the clutch of between four and seven glossy white eggs is complete. The male and female both incubate the clutch, each spending as little as 30 minutes in the nest before the other takes over. As the days progress, the birds change places with decreasing regularity. The

Following fledging of the chicks, family parties of great spotted woodpeckers will remain together for several weeks. The male and female share the task of feeding the young birds.

male usually occupies the nest at night, while the female roosts in another hole nearby.

While the woodpeckers are busy incubating their brood, a considerable change is taking place in the surrounding woodlands. With the warmth of spring, leaves and buds burst forth. The pale green canopy provides shade for the woodpecker's nest site, although this is rarely located on the sunnier south side of the tree, and the growing vegetation brings about a transformation in the insect world. Many moths emerge and lay their eggs, with the resulting abundance of caterpillars and larvae arriving just in time for the woodpeckers to feed their newly hatched young.

Raising the chicks

Woodpecker chicks are fed by both adults on a diet of caterpillars picked from the foliage. With a huge beakful of food, the male disappears into the nest to feed the tiny, helpless chicks. Afterwards, he may nestle the youngsters until the female calls from a nearby tree to signal that she now has food for the chicks.

When both parents are away foraging, the young woodpeckers huddle together

GREAT SPOTTED WOODPECKER CALENDAR

JANUARY • FEBRUARY

The lengthening days encourage the birds to begin drumming to attract mates.
The male advertises his territory, while the female drums to encourage the male to accept her presence nearby.

MARCH • APRIL

Aggression erupts as wandering birds try to oust territory-holding males or their mates. Pairs are established and nest excavation begins, or refurbishment if the birds are using a previous year's nest.

MAY • JUNE

Eggs are usually laid in early May and hatch after about 15 days. Parents are busy gleaning insects from tree foliage for their growing broods. The young fledge around mid-to-late June at 22–24 days old.

JULY • AUGUST

The adults often divide their fledged young into two groups, caring for half of the brood each. Two to three weeks after leaving the nest, the young will become independent. The moult period begins in mid-July.

SEPTEMBER • OCTOBER

In autumn, as insect prey diminishes in the cooling, shortening days, ripening hazelnuts, beechmast and acorns form a major part of the birds' diet. By mid-September, the moult is complete.

NOVEMBER • DECEMBER

As autumn harvests are exhausted, wood-boring beetles and their larvae become a valuable source of food Woodpeckers also visit birdfeeders more frequently in these hard months.

Over the past decade, great spotted woodpeckers have become familiar visitors to garden birdfeeders. Their bills are ideally suited to the extraction of peanuts from within mesh containers.

REMARKABLE WRYNECK

Classified in a separate subfamily, the wryneck is an unusual woodpecker. Its common name arose from its habit of twisting and turning its neck at odd angles when startled. In witchcraft, wrynecks were used to cast spells against an enemy and their scientific name of *Jynx torquilla* is the source of the expression to 'put a jinx' on someone.

Once a reasonably common and widespread breeding bird, the wryneck is now seen only as a migrant in the British Isles, following a steady decline from the early 20th century onward. The reasons for its demise are still not completely understood. It is thought that ants – one of the birds' favourite foods – have been badly affected by pesticides in lowland areas, but this does not explain the decline in Scotland.

In the late 1960s and early 1970s, a small number of pairs bred tentatively in the Scottish Highlands, but hopes that wryneck numbers would be restored were dashed when the birds disappeared again in the early 1980s.

A subtle blend of muted tones gives the wryneck superb camouflage both on the ground and against tree trunks. Migrant birds are most likely to be seen in coastal areas from August to October.

for warmth, as they are very sensitive to the cold. The adults continue to feed the nestlings throughout the day, with clear peaks in feeding in the early morning and late afternoon and something of a quiet spell around noon.

As their feathers and strength develop, the chicks take it in turns to cling just beneath the entrance hole, in the hope of being first to secure the next incoming meal. The parents continue to brood the chicks during the day for about 12 days, and during the night until about two days before they fledge.

At this time, sibling rivalry can be very intense as the chicks compete for food. Squabbles are often severe and can even end in death. During their last few days in the nest, the young are fed at its entrance, where they call loudly and incessantly from dawn to dusk. The noise frequently attracts attention, but if the parents detect potential danger they give a scolding call. The young promptly cease calling and retreat to the bottom of the nest.

Leaving home

When the youngsters are 20 to 24 days old, the parents encourage them to fledge by waiting with food in nearby trees. If a hesitant youngster does not go voluntarily, it may well be pushed from behind by a more enthusiastic sibling.

For the first night or two, the young woodpeckers roost by clinging to a trunk or branch. This leaves them vulnerable to predators, so they rapidly acquire the habit of roosting in a tree hole. Soon after the chicks have fledged, the adults divide the brood into two groups. Each group is attended by one parent for a further two or more weeks.

By the time the young leave to find their own territories, the adult birds have already begun their annual moult, which may take three or more months to complete. The first tinge of autumn signals the start of the season of plenty in the woodland. Acorns, seeds and fruits are devoured with relish as each ripens in turn. The woodpeckers return to a solitary existence throughout the harshest months, often visiting birdfeeders and adding a flash of colour to dull winter gardens.

WILDLIFE WATCH

Where can I see great spotted woodpeckers?

● Almost any sizeable British woodland, except in the far north of Scotland, will support great spotted woodpeckers. The birds prefer broad-leaved woodlands, because of the abundance of insects and fruits, although they do live in conifer woodlands, especially in the Scottish Highlands. Here, however, the density of woodpeckers is lower.

● The great spotted is the most common of the three woodpecker species that reside in the New Forest. Epping Forest in Essex, the Mens woodland near Petworth in West Sussex, the Forest of Dean in Gloucestershire, Cannock Chase in Staffordshire, the Peak District, the Lake District and the valley woods of mid-Wales are among the best places to look for woodpeckers.

● One good way to attract great spotted woodpeckers to your garden is by smearing fat, lard or suet onto cracks in tree bark – or onto a cut branch or plank nailed to a fence.

Female great spotted woodpeckers lack the red nape patch of the males.

Recognising finches

An attractive group of birds, finches enliven woodlands, countryside and gardens as well as urban areas. In spring, the colourful breeding plumage of the males of most finch species is at its brightest.

Visit almost anywhere in Britain where seed-producing plants are common and you are likely to find finches present for at least part of the year. As a group, these small birds mostly have a stout-bodied appearance and they can be recognised by their typically forked tails, short conical bills and bounding flight.

Outside the breeding season, most finches form flocks. While in the majority of cases these gatherings involve a single species, mixed flocks often occur when the habits and preferred foods of the group members are similar.

Finches are passerines – perching birds – and many of them exploit their agility to the full when feeding. Even those species that feed low down usually take to the trees when alarmed.

A characteristic of most passerines is their singing – hence the alternative name of 'songbirds' – but among British finches only the chaffinch, greenfinch, linnet, siskin and goldfinch have songs worthy of the name. The repertoire of the other species comprises either simple twittering notes, or other sounds that are more like calls than songs.

Specialist bills

Finches have a range of bill sizes and shapes that have evolved to suit particular diets. At one end of the scale is the hawfinch, with a bill so massive it can crack cherry stones. At the other is the goldfinch, which has a slender, pointed bill to extract teasel seeds from between seed-head spikes. Oddest of all is the crossbill's overlapping beak – well adapted for extracting seeds from pine cones.

The bullfinch is a secretive bird. Both male and female (seen here) perch in the open only briefly, generally preferring to hide in dense cover.

WILDLIFE WATCH

Where can I see finches?

● Most finch species are associated with woodlands in the breeding season. Open country finches, such as linnets and twites, are easier to see at this time of year. The best way to find them is to learn their calls and songs.

● In winter, look for finches in flocks. Species such as bramblings and chaffinches often feed on the woodland floor, while siskins, redpolls and crossbills feed in the trees. Stubble fields are also good for a few finch species, where they may mix with buntings.

EASY GUIDE TO SPOTTING FINCHES

Chaffinch (male)

Brambling (male)

Greenfinch (male)

Goldfinch

Siskin (male)

Twite

Redpoll

Linnet (male)

Bullfinch (male)

Hawfinch

Crossbill (male)

WHAT ARE FINCHES?

● Finches are passerine birds of the family Fringillidae. They are small birds with proportionately thick bills.

● Primarily seed-eaters, finches catch invertebrates in summer, particularly insects and spiders, to feed growing chicks.

● Many of the finch species are associated with wooded terrain, especially in spring and summer.

HOW CAN I IDENTIFY FINCHES?

● Calls and songs are one way to track down breeding birds in spring. Members of winter flocks keep in contact by means of calls.

● Some finches have distinctive plumage features, such as the bullfinch's white rump, the goldfinch's single broad yellow wingbars and the greenfinch's olive green back.

● Siskins and redpolls often feed together in birch or alder.

● Chaffinches reveal white wingbars in flight, but look closely at a flock and you may spot the bold white rump of a brambling among flying birds.

● Linnets and twites are very similar little brown birds. Listen for the twite's distinctive, nasal '*twaaait*' calls. Twites also have yellow, not grey, bills in winter.

● The shape of the bill in a hawfinch or crossbill is enough to allow certain identification.

Distribution map key

☐ Not present

■ Present all year round

☐ Present during winter months

☐ Present during summer months

CHAFFINCH *Fringilla coelebs*

The male chaffinch has mostly pinkish underparts with a blue-grey crown and nape. The back is chestnut, the rump green and the wings have black and white bars. The male's bill, dull pink-grey for most of the year, turns blue in spring. Females have a similar wing pattern to males, but a duller brown body colour. Juveniles resemble them, but have a buff, not green, rump.

● SIZE
Length 14.5cm (6in)

● NEST
Very neat cup in fork of tree – outer layer of lichens, spider webs; inner of grass, moss; lining of feathers, hair or rootlets.

● BREEDING
Lays 4–5 bluish or grey eggs with darker spots and marks in April–June

● FOOD
Seeds; invertebrates in summer

● HABITAT
Woodlands, farmland, scrub, parks and gardens

● VOICE
Sharp '*pink*' calls; song a descending trill with final flourish

● DISTRIBUTION
Very common and widespread over almost all of Britain and Ireland

Tail black with white outer feathers

Pale olive brown

Blue-grey crown and pinkish face

Orange-pink breast

Female

Male

Birdwatchers often overlook the chaffinch in favour of more unusual species, even though the male especially is an attractive bird.

BRAMBLING *Fringilla montifringilla*

The white rump and orange breast and shoulder patch enable the male bird to be easily recognised. In winter, the upperparts darken and appear scaly and the bill is yellow with a black tip. By spring, the bill is black. Females have the same bold wing pattern as males, but are duller, with a plainer head – the male's is speckled or mottled with black. Juveniles resemble females.

● **SIZE**
Length 14cm (5½in)

● **NEST**
Cup of grass, moss and lichen in fork high in tree

● **BREEDING**
Lays 5–7 greenish to buff, spotted eggs in May–June

● **FOOD**
Seeds, especially beechmast in autumn; invertebrates in summer

● **HABITAT**
Northern birch forests in summer; open ground and woodland edges, especially beech woods, in winter

● **VOICE**
Rasping *'tsweep'* calls; louder, nasal *'tseh-ep'* of alarm; brief, hard *'tyeck'* flight call; male spring song monotonous, nasal

● **DISTRIBUTION**
Winter visitor and passage migrant in spring and autumn; numbers depend on weather and food in northern Europe

The brambling's plumage varies according to sex and time of year (this is a female in winter), but all birds have a combination of orange breast and white rump at all times.

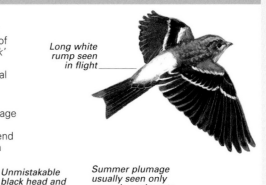

Long white rump seen in flight

Unmistakable black head and bright breast

Summer plumage usually seen only on spring migrants

Male Summer

Orange breast duller in winter

Underparts white

Male Winter

GREENFINCH *Carduelis chloris*

The greenfinch is olive green with patches of yellow in its wings and a forked tail that shows clearly in flight. The flight feathers and base of the tail are dark blackish brown. The bill is short, but heavy and pale ivory or pinkish. Females are similar to males but duller, with faint streaks on the crown and upperparts. Juveniles are less colourful and more streaked.

● **SIZE**
Length 15cm (6in)

● **NEST**
Large, untidy cup of grasses and mosses built in dense cover

● **BREEDING**
Lays 4–6 greyish, whitish or pale buff, lightly dark-speckled eggs in April–July

● **FOOD**
Mainly large seeds; a few invertebrates

● **HABITAT**
Mixed woodlands, hedgerows, parks and gardens

● **VOICE**
Twittering calls, and rising *'tsoooeet'* of alarm; song of 2 types, a long, nasal *'breeeeze'* falling in pitch, or a mix of twittering and trilling

● **DISTRIBUTION**
Common and widespread resident across most of Britain and Ireland

Greenfinches are often associated with tall hedgerows, both in the countryside and in gardens. They favour dense cover for nesting and roosting in winter.

Yellow at base of tail

Yellow on flight feathers evident in flight

Strikingly olive green and yellow

Dull and heavily streaked

Juvenile

Male

GOLDFINCH *Carduelis carduelis*

Small and very colourful, the goldfinch has a red and white face, black head, warm buff upperparts and black wings that have broad yellow bands. The underparts are pale buff, the belly white. Sexes are almost identical, but males have slightly more red on the face. Juveniles resemble adults, but do not develop the head markings for two months after fledging.

● SIZE
Length 12cm (5in)

● NEST
Tiny neat cup of moss, lichen, grass and other material lined with hair, plant down and feathers; concealed in dense bush

● BREEDING
Lays 4–6 pale blue, rusty or purplish brown spotted eggs in April–July

● FOOD
Small seeds, especially soft, half-ripe seeds of teasels, groundsels, dandelions and thistles

● HABITAT
Open country with trees or shrubs, gardens, parks, woodland edges, scrub, waste ground

● VOICE
Sweet sounding, liquid *'switt-witt-witt'* and short canary-like twittering song

● DISTRIBUTION
Widespread resident across most of Britain and Ireland apart from far north

Yellow wingbars seen in flight

Striking black, red and white markings on adult head

Juvenile

No adult face pattern for first two months

Male

Goldfinch flocks – also known as 'charms' – are drawn to patches of teasel and thistles. The birds' bills are long and thin enough to extract the seeds.

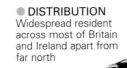

SISKIN *Carduelis spinus*

A dainty bird, the siskin has black wings, each crossed by two broad yellow bars. The male is bright yellow-green above with a black forehead, crown and chin. The black tail is forked and has bright yellow patches along the edges. The small, yellowish bill is sharply pointed. Females are streakier and lack the male's black head markings. Juveniles are browner and even more streaked.

● SIZE
Length 12cm (5in)

● NEST
Tiny neat cup of twigs, mosses, grass and other material, lined with hair and other soft material; sited high in conifer tree

● BREEDING
Lays 3–5 blue, red-brown spotted eggs in April–July

● FOOD
Seeds, particularly spruce, birch and alder

● HABITAT
Coniferous forests, riverside alders and birches; gardens in winter and early spring

● VOICE
Clear metallic *'tzu'*, wheezy *'tzoo-eet'*, often mixed with hard twittering; sharp *'tsewi'* flight-call; sweet twittering song often ending with long, nasal note

● DISTRIBUTION
Increasingly common resident over most of Britain and Ireland; most common in north

Black wings with double broad yellow wingbars

Female lacks male's black crown

Yellow on female is duller than on male

Female

Black forehead, crown and chin

Yellow underparts grade to streaky white

Tail black and forked

Male

Although superficially similar to a greenfinch, a siskin can be distinguished by its smaller size and double yellow wingbars. Adult males have striking black crowns.

T W I T E   *Carduelis flavirostris*

The twite is rather a plain finch, with dark, streaked plumage and a short bill, which is grey in summer and yellow in winter. The male's pink rump is distinctive, but seen well only in flight. Pale wingbars and outer tail feathers are also visible in good light. The sexes are similar, but females have brownish rumps. Juveniles are similar to winter adults.

● **SIZE**
Length 14cm (5½in)

● **NEST**
Bulky cup of twigs, grass, bracken and other materials densely lined with hair and wool; hidden in bracken, bush, bark, or among rocks or stones in wall

● **BREEDING**
Lays 4–6 blue, red-to-purple speckled eggs in May–June

● **FOOD**
Small seeds, usually collected from ground

● **HABITAT**
Treeless open country; overwinters mainly on coastal marshes, shores and adjacent fields

● **VOICE**
Nasal *'chweek'* and twittering flight song

● **DISTRIBUTION**
Breeds in Scotland and in smaller numbers in northern England, Wales and Ireland; overwinters further south

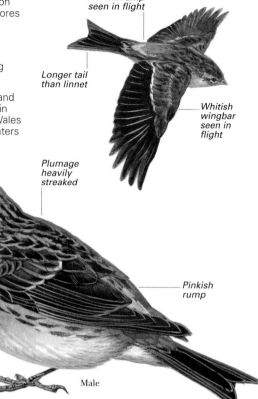

Pink rump seen in flight

Longer tail than linnet

Whitish wingbar seen in flight

Plumage heavily streaked

Bill grey in summer but yellow in winter

Pinkish rump

Male

During the breeding season, twites favour comparatively bleak, open moorland habitats. Wire fences often provide the best places for the birds to perch.

R E D P O L L   *Carduelis flammea*

The upperparts of this little finch are streaked brown, as are the flanks of the pale underparts. The male has a black chin, small red fore-crown, partial white eyebrow and a rosy breast in the breeding season. Females lack the pink breast and have a smaller, black-edged red fore-crown. Juveniles lack a red crown and are more streaked.

● **SIZE**
Length 11.5–14cm (4½–5½in)

● **NEST**
Untidy cup of grass, moss, old flower heads and other material lined with hair and soft material; sited high in a tall shrub or tree

● **BREEDING**
Lays 4–5 blue, reddish or purplish speckled eggs in late April–June

● **FOOD**
Mostly small seeds, especially birch and alder

● **HABITAT**
Birch and alder woods, conifer plantations; also tall hedgerows, heaths with scattered trees, and alder, willow and hawthorn scrub

● **VOICE**
High-pitched *'chuchuchu'* calls; plaintive *'tsooo-eet'* alarm call; song a mixture of buzzing trills and calls

● **DISTRIBUTION**
Widespread across Britain and Ireland, but recent decline. Distribution and numbers vary greatly from year to year

Two white wingbars show in flight

Uniformly streaked with brown

Red forehead and black chin

Juvenile

Streaked pinkish rump in breeding season

Male

Redpolls are usually found feeding in trees. Only in harsh weather are they enticed to the ground by spilt grain.

LINNET *Carduelis cannabina*

A chestnut back, dark flight feathers and tail, and a grey head with a crimson forehead characterise the male linnet. The chin is white with dark streaks and the crimson breast merges into pale underparts. Females are browner above and paler below with no crimson. In flight, both show white wing and tail patches. Juveniles resemble the more heavily streaked females.

During the breeding season, male linnets are often seen perched on prominent look-outs. In winter, the species forms large feeding flocks.

- **SIZE**
  Length 13.5cm (5½in)
- **NEST**
  Cup of twigs, rootlets, grasses, lined with hair or wool; built low in thorny bush
- **BREEDING**
  Lays 4–6 pale blue, dark-blotched eggs in April–June
- **FOOD**
  Seeds; a few insects in summer
- **HABITAT**
  Open country with scrub patches and hedgerows; waste ground, farmland and coastal marshes in winter

- **VOICE**
  Plaintive '*tsooo-eet*' alarm call; fast, soft, twittering flight call; song sweet twittering mixed with metallic or scratchy notes
- **DISTRIBUTION**
  Widespread resident across most of Britain, apart from north-west and Ireland

Whitish wing flashes

White at tail base

Red cap acquired after one year

More darkly streaked than male

Female

Chestnut back and crimson chest patches

Male

Tail forked

BULLFINCH *Pyrrhula pyrrhula*

The male bullfinch is brightly coloured, reddish pink below and blue-grey above, with black cap, chin, flight feathers and tail, and a prominent white rump. Broad white bars show on folded wings and in flight. Females are similarly patterned, but brownish grey above and pinkish grey below. Juveniles resemble females, but are browner and lack the black cap.

The combination of a blue-grey mantle, glossy black cap and bright rosy breast ensure the male bullfinch is unmistakable.

- **SIZE**
  Length 15cm (6in)
- **NEST**
  Flimsy platform of twigs, moss and lichen; neat inner cup of hair and rootlets; sited in dense bush
- **BREEDING**
  Lays 3–6 pale green-blue or blue eggs in May–July
- **FOOD**
  Mainly tree buds, also tree flowers, berries, seeds; a few invertebrates in breeding season

- **HABITAT**
  Thick scrub, woodland edges, dense hedgerows, orchards and gardens
- **VOICE**
  Distinctive, melancholy, low, soft but far-carrying, piping '*den*' calls; song (rarely heard) a quiet creaking warble
- **DISTRIBUTION**
  Widespread across most of mainland Britain and Ireland

White rump conspicuous in flight

Black cap

Short white wingbar

Bluish grey nape and mantle

Short and stubby black bill

Mainly black wings with prominent white wingbar

Rosy pink underparts

Male

HAWFINCH *Coccothraustes coccothraustes*

A large bird, the hawfinch looks top-heavy in profile due to its massive bill. In flight and when perched, it appears very short-tailed and the wings show large areas of white. The male has an orange-buff head and pinkish buff breast, with dark flight feathers and broadly white-tipped tail. Females are similar but duller. Juveniles have dark-barred underparts.

● SIZE
Length 18cm (7in)

● NEST
Flimsy, sparsely lined platform of twigs, grasses, rootlets, lichen; sited high in a tree

● BREEDING
Lays 4–6 pale blue or greenish eggs with blackish markings in April–June

● FOOD
Large tree seeds and fruit stones; some insects in summer

● HABITAT
Deciduous and mixed woodland; parks, orchards and large gardens with mature trees, especially hornbeams

● VOICE
Loud, explosive *'pzic'* calls

● DISTRIBUTION
Scarce breeding bird, usually found in small colonies, mainly in south-east England, with a few in Wales, northern England and Scotland

Black bib and black at base of bill

Large triangular bill

Striking white wingbars

Male

A huge bill is the hawfinch's best identification feature, useful for cracking hard-cased seeds and cherry stones. In winter, these birds often feed on the ground.

Brown with short bars on underparts

Juvenile

Short tail

COMMON CROSSBILL *Loxia curvirostra*

Mainly brick-red plumage distinguishes the dumpy male common crossbill. Wings and tail are dark but the rump is bright and shows well in flight. Females are green with darker wings and a brighter rump. Both sexes have distinctive crossed mandibles. Juveniles have brown, streaked plumage and sometimes show indistinct pale wingbars.

● SIZE
Length 16.5cm (6½in)

● NEST
Twiggy platform with cup of grass, moss, lichen and bark lined with hair, feathers and moss; sited high in conifer near main trunk of tree

● BREEDING
Lays 3–4 whitish, dark-spotted eggs in February–May

● FOOD
Mainly conifer seeds, especially spruce, also larch and pine

● HABITAT
Coniferous forests

● VOICE
Main call is a sharp *'chip chip chip'*; song a mixture of soft trills, loud creaks and warbling

● DISTRIBUTION
Widespread, but not common, in conifer forests across Britain and Ireland

Broad-based wings

Reddish plumage

Mandibles overlap at the tips

Yellowish green plumage

Male

Dark wings

Female

The crossbill is a squat finch with a large head and a stout crossed bill unique to the group. In winter, it forms flocks that are invariably found in conifer woods.

Centipedes and millipedes

Most frequently seen scuttling for the shadows when surprised by a torch-beam or sudden light, centipedes and millipedes have more legs than any other living creatures.

Although mainly nocturnal and hence rarely seen, centipedes and millipedes are, in fact, extremely numerous and live all over the country. They are both members of a group of invertebrates called the Myriapoda, meaning 'many feet', and share the same basic body plan of a head attached to a number of identical body segments. Centipedes have a single pair of legs on each body segment, while millipedes have two pairs of legs per segment. In general, centipedes are more flattened than millipedes and their legs are longer in relation to their body width. Other differences lie in diet, defence mechanisms and breeding habits.

Different diets

Centipedes are carnivorous, hunting by using their sense of touch and by picking up vibrations from the movement of their prey. Most British centipedes have very poor eyesight, and many are entirely blind. Their diet consists largely of worms, insect larvae and other soft-bodied invertebrates, some of which are garden pests. As a result centipedes are, on the whole, looked upon favourably by gardeners.

On its head, the centipede has a pair of claws modified into fangs, with which it injects poison to stun prey. The venom is produced in small sacs inside the claws and squeezed through a tiny hole near the end of each claw as it pierces the prey's body, swiftly and effectively immobilising the victim. No British species is large enough to deliver a bite that could harm a human, but some tropical centipedes are so big that they can cause a very painful wound that is sometimes fatal to children.

In contrast, millipedes are mainly vegetarian, and have much smaller and weaker jaws than centipedes. Mostly they feed on dead and decaying plant matter,

Members of the pill millipede family are far shorter, and have far fewer pairs of legs, than most millipedes. They roll themselves up into an armoured ball for protection.

DID YOU KNOW?

Millipedes live longer than many other invertebrates. The male common pill millipede, for example, does not become sexually mature until between two and three years of age, while the female takes a further year to reach this stage in development. Following sexual maturity, they may then live up to the age of 10 or 11.

▲ Soil centipedes are most often seen when digging the garden. Their long, thin bodies enable them to use earthworm burrows to make their way through the soil, and the worms also form part of their diet.

▶ The snake millipede coils up defensively when it feels threatened. This pose is adopted by many species when attacked by predators, as it protects the vulnerable head at the centre of the spiral.

but a number do feed on living plant tissues and can make a nuisance of themselves by attacking crops.

Coordinating movement

The British species of snake centipede, a soil dweller, has up to 101 pairs of legs, a number matched by the common woodland snake millipede. Even these pale into insignificance beside some tropical millipedes, which may have as many as 200 pairs of legs.

These creatures are remarkably efficient at coordinating their appendages. Movement of the legs passes in waves, from back to front, along the length of the body – the more pairs of legs, the greater the number of waves and the animal appears to undulate along the woodland floor.

As centipedes generally have longer legs than millipedes, they can move much faster, their bodies undulating from side to side as they run. Those that live in the soil either follow burrows made by other soil-dwelling creatures, such as worms, or move through natural fissures. The long, slim snake centipedes are unusual in being able to walk backwards as well as forwards – no doubt this ability is a great help when coming to a dead-end in a soil fissure. The larger soil-living snake millipedes, however, bulldoze their

cylindrical bodies through the earth, pushing with their many legs to force the soil particles aside.

Survival strategies

Both centipedes and millipedes are at risk of becoming a meal for larger animals, such as frogs and toads, birds, shrews and spiders. The soil-dwelling species are protected from attack by such creatures, but those that move around on the surface need some means of defence. Centipedes usually rely on their ability to move fast to escape from danger, while the slower-moving millipedes make use of two different ploys to avoid being eaten.

Many millipedes produce unpleasant or poisonous secretions when attacked. These can repel many, but not all, predators, a number of their enemies having become immune to such secretions. An alternative defence is to roll up in a tight ball so that the delicate and vulnerable undersides are protected by the amour-plated rings encircling the upper part of each segment. Long-bodied snake millipedes curl their body into a spiral with the head at its centre, while pill millipedes can roll themselves into an armoured ball, leaving none of the vulnerable parts of the body uncovered. The ability to hide the head completely distinguishes pill millipedes from woodlice, many of which can also roll into a ball but they leave the head exposed.

Courtship and breeding

Centipedes share a brief form of courtship before they mate, which may involve the courting couple circling for some minutes, tapping one

▶ The white-legged snake millipede favours the damper, darker, mossy parts of woods where it is less likely to dehydrate.

LIVING WITH MYRIAPODS

Centipedes and millipedes are mainly nocturnal, so it is not often that the average householder comes across one. There are occasions, however, when snake millipedes and flattened brown centipedes show a tendency to wander and accidentally find their way into houses by crawling under an outside door.

They are all completely harmless and should be carefully placed back outdoors where they belong.

A few millipedes, such as the spotted snake millipede, have been suspected of attacking crops. Most often they are found curled up in cavities in potato tubers. Whether they cause the

damage in the first place or are just making use of an opening dug by another creature, such as a slug, is uncertain.

More seriously, some millipedes have been found feeding on the roots of sugar beet crops, and it seems that here they are the culprits – their depredations can cause severe damage to the crop.

BRITISH CENTIPEDES AND MILLIPEDES

There are about 45 species of centipede in the British Isles, and about 50 of millipedes. All are rather small and drab, unlike many of the brightly coloured, often large, tropical species. Individual species are difficult to recognise without the aid of a microscope and a specialist guide to identification.

The centipedes most likely to be found in the British Isles belong to four main groups or orders:

● Snake centipedes are long and slim, pale yellow to reddish brown in colour. They are blind, soil-dwelling animals with 37–101 body segments.

● Scolopendromorph centipedes are shorter, more robust creatures with just 20 body segments. This group includes the exotic giant centipedes characteristic of warmer regions of the world, which may occasionally appear in this country when imported accidentally with fruit such as bananas. British scolopendromorph centipedes are all small and blind. Only one is native, the other two were introduced by man at some time in the past.

● Stone-dwelling centipedes, called lithobiomorphs, are the most commonly encountered of native species, with robust, shiny-brown, flattened, 15-segmented bodies,

usually with three pairs of simple eyes on the head. They are often seen scuttling away at great speed when a stone or log is lifted. One species, Lithobius variegatus, is restricted to the British Isles. Lamyctes fulvicornis resembles Lithobius but is distinguished by its single pair of simple eyes and ability to curl up when disturbed. It is widely distributed elsewhere, but its main claim to fame in Britain is that all specimens are female; they reproduce parthenogenetically, that is without mating.

● House centipedes are long-legged, active and fast-running with 15 segments, and much longer back than front legs. Just one species, the European house centipede, Scutigera coleoptrata, is found in Britain in the Channel Islands, where it may be indigenous. It occasionally turns up as an accidental import on the mainland, but is more likely to be seen scuttling around on the walls of Mediterranean houses in search of insect prey.

Millipedes are represented by three orders:

● Pill millipedes have 11 or 12 arched segments and can roll into a ball.

● Flat-backed millipedes have 19 or 20 flattened segments with noticeable lateral extensions or 'keels'.

● Snake millipedes are roughly cylindrical in cross section, with up to 50 segments.

▲ Groups of woodland snake millipedes often spend daylight hours clustered together beneath the bark of a tree. They normally emerge at dusk to feed on dead or decaying vegetation.

◄ Flat-backed millipedes may be found in woodlands and wilder gardens. They seek shelter in dark and damp retreats, such as beneath stones and flower pots.

▲ The curved, pointed poison fangs of the brown centipede are clearly visible on either side of the head.

another with their antennae. The male then spins a tiny pad of silk, deposits a package of sperm on the pad, and leaves it for the female to locate on her own. Due to poor or non-existent eyesight, it may be some hours before she eventually succeeds. Finding the sperm droplet with her antennae, she crawls over it, wipes her rear end on it and sweeps it up into her body. Millipedes have more intimate mating habits, wrapping around each other for up to several hours while the male uses adapted legs to introduce the sperm directly into his mate.

Most female centipedes and millipedes make some form of nest in which to lay eggs. Several species of centipedes attend diligently to their eggs until the young hatch and are ready to disperse. Soil-dwelling snake centipedes, for example, lie with their bodies curled around their eggs and will defend them against attacks from other centipedes. The eggs are also cleaned regularly, removing fungal spores that could otherwise germinate and destroy them.

Millipedes hatch with only three pairs of legs, gradually adding extra body sections and legs as they go through a succession of moults, shedding and reforming their hard outer skeleton. Most centipedes hatch with a full complement of legs, but the stone-dwelling species are born with six pairs and must also grow new legs through a series of moults.

▲ The red-striped snake millipede is one of the most attractive species. Although it mainly searches the woodland floor for food, in damp weather it may climb plants to nibble fruit.

◄ In Britain, the house centipede is restricted to the Channel Isles, but it is common throughout southern Europe, where it may often be seen indoors running rapidly over walls and floors. Its very long hind legs overrun the front legs when moving at speed and are clearly visible.

▼ The most commonly encountered species is the brown centipede. Although nocturnal, the occasional individual may wander through the cool depths of an English woodland during the day.

WILDLIFE WATCH

Where can I see centipedes and millipedes?

● Centipedes and millipedes lack the waxy waterproof layer on the outside of the body that has contributed to the success of so many insects, so they lose water easily. As a result they shun bright light and are mainly nocturnal or live in dark, moist conditions such as beneath stones or bark, in leaf-litter or in the soil. This is where they can usually be found.

● Many species come out at night in search of food. Snake millipedes may be found walking up house walls, while the big, brown Lithobius centipedes, out hunting for prey, may sometimes be picked out in the light of a torch before they scuttle rapidly away to find a crevice in which to hide.

Orange-tip butterfly

Often seen fluttering along hedgerows and through sunny woodland rides, the male orange-tip butterfly spends the spring months in a ceaseless quest to find and mate with a female of the species.

One of the first butterflies to emerge from its chrysalis, the orange-tip appears in early spring and the sight of a lively male dancing among the roadside vegetation is a sure sign that winter is over.

This bright little member of the familiar 'cabbage white' family, the Pieridae, gets its name from the vivid orange patches on the male's forewings, which are otherwise mainly white. These patches clearly stand out when the butterfly is perched or as it flutters past. The female's wings are also mainly white but with grey or black tips, which are small and rounded like the male's. Both have a black spot on each forewing and distinctive mottled green undersides.

Changing distribution

The orange-tip is found across most of the British Isles and Ireland. Absent only from mountainous regions and parts of northern Scotland, its wide distribution is partly due to its roving lifestyle. The orange-tip is probably still most common in the southern half of Britain and southern Ireland, although numbers have declined in these areas in recent years and there has been an expansion of its northern range. One reason is that modern farming practices have affected one of the caterpillars' main foodplants,

The male orange-tip is one of the most colourful indicators of spring. At rest, the undersides of its wings look as though they have been sponge-dabbed with green and yellow paint, and provide effective camouflage.

Unlike the brightly coloured males, female orange-tips have only a smoky grey patch at the leading edge of their forewings. The female emerges from the chrysalis slightly later than the male.

the cuckoo flower (lady's smock), and caused the butterfly to rely much more on garlic mustard, which thrives in hedgerows and roadside verges only with careful management.

On the wing

The orange-tip is on the wing from late April into June, its wanderings taking it to a variety of habitats in search of its chosen foodplants. Damp, flowery meadows, herbaceous verges and waysides are preferred, but the orange-tip may also be seen along woodland rides and clearings, at the perimeters of farmland and in gardens. Unlike its plainer relatives – the large and small whites – it is no threat to allotments and gardeners can enjoy its visits without fearing for their vegetables.

Male orange-tips are more energetic than females and, being brighter in

colour, they seem to be more numerous. When the wings of either sex are folded, the delicate dappled green underside is exposed. This provides effective camouflage when the butterfly is resting on cow parsley or other such favoured perches, and also distinguishes the female from other white butterflies. The orange-tip is so confident in its camouflage that it will settle in the open overnight or in poor weather, sitting proud and exposed on top of cuckoo flowers in rush-filled meadows.

The males are relentless fliers and a little morning sun soon rouses them for their patrols. In May, the verges burst with cow parsley, greater stitchwort and garlic mustard and males explore hedge-banks, country lanes and lush margins. Fluttering along above the vegetation, they make regular diversions and detours

Like other butterflies, the orange-tip's compound eyes are made up of many small facets. These are too small to see without a hand lens, but their reflective surfaces create the illusion of bands of colour.

to investigate flowers and other butterflies. If a patrolling male meets a rival, a brief skirmish may take place. These chases appear to be more a game of 'follow-my-leader' than a heated dogfight and the males soon continue on their separate ways. Orange-tips are wandering insects – they do not defend a territory or remain attached to one particular site. However, prime habitats can support good numbers of butterflies, forming a dispersed colony.

Single eggs

Female orange-tips remain hidden in cover for longer periods than males and are probably easiest to watch when laying their eggs. Once they have mated, females

tour the vicinity, homing in on garlic mustard and cuckoo flower. The flowers of these plants can be busy places, with wandering aphids, ants and weevils, but the orange-tip is more at risk from the crab spiders that wait under the flower, or spin strands of silk across the flower head.

Orange-tips lay their eggs in a variety of sites. Open meadows, sunny clearings and shaded woodland are all used. The female alights on a flower and curls her tail underneath its petals to lay a single elongated, ribbed egg on the short flower stalk. Laying a single egg on each plant she visits ensures that each caterpillar, which will hatch a week or so later, will

Most adult orange-tips probably live no longer than three weeks, but since emergence is staggered, the 'orange-tip season' lasts for eight weeks or more.

have enough food without needing to share with other caterpillars. The eggs are pale green at first but soon turn orange. The hatchling caterpillars are a dull green, specked with short black bristles that look like spots at first glance. Later in the summer, when they are fully grown, they cocoon themselves as chrysalises and those that survive the winter will be ready to emerge the following spring.

WILDLIFE WATCH

Where can I see orange-tip butterflies?

● Compared to those of most butterflies, orange-tip eggs are fairly easy to find on short flower stalks, just below the flower head, in woodlands and meadows. Take a regular walk in May and you might be able to follow the progress of the caterpillar as it grows through a number of moults. Put a small marker tag on the plant to help you locate it on each visit.

● If you have a sunny spot in your garden, try encouraging orange-tips to visit by planting some suitable foodplants on which the females can lay their eggs – close clumps of honesty, garlic mustard and cuckoo flower. Watch to find out which species is the orange-tips' favourite.

● Set up a simple local climate monitoring scheme. Keep a note of the first date you see orange-tip butterflies, then see how this varies from year to year.

RACE AGAINST TIME

Orange-tip caterpillars ponderously explore the foodplant on which they hatch, feeding on the seed pods. They must grow very quickly before they run out of suitable food. The seed pods are also growing and ripening fast, and will soon drop their seeds and die back. By July, the caterpillars must be fully grown and ready for the next challenge.

Each orange-tip spends most of its year-long life as a chrysalis – it must survive in this form from late July or August to the following April or early May. In order to find a safe sheltered place to pupate, the caterpillar goes 'walkabout', often ending up in nearby scrub. Winter flooding, cattle grazing, verge mowing and trampling are routine hazards and it is testimony to the care with which the caterpillar selects its resting place that so many survive.

The orange-tip chrysalis may be brown or sometimes green, and is pointed and well camouflaged, closely resembling a fruit or a broken stalk.

As it grows, the caterpillar turns greyish green in colour. A white stripe along each side aids concealment by breaking up the caterpillar's outline as it nibbles its way along leaves and seed pods.

Anemones and relatives

Scattered among woodlands, marshes and limestone hills, anemones and related wild flowers bring colour from early spring onward. Some have a pungent odour while others, best left untouched, have poisonous sap.

A large number of British wild flowers, including wood anemones, hellebores, monkshood and columbine, all belong to the same family – the Ranunculaceae. Most of these plants have attractive flowers that are complex in form and often arranged in conspicuous clusters, with colours ranging from violet to bright yellow. It is perhaps surprising that

buttercups – known for their simple, cup-shaped flowers – are members of the same family as these elaborate plants. In fact, the basic flower is similar in all of them – bowl-shaped with five outer green flower parts (sepals) and five inner coloured petals, although the distinction between sepals and petals is not always clear.

Specialised blooms
Primitive flowers that evolved in the time of the dinosaurs were unspecialised, often solitary and symmetric with a basic set of floral parts. Buttercups, anemones and pheasant's-eye retain this simple form, but others are more complex. Monkshood, for example, has flowers massed into spikes. Columbine has long, nectar-filled spurs to attract insects. Such flowers have evolved a long way from their buttercup-like ancestors.

Some of the flowers have nectar-secreting glands, called nectaries, at the base of the petals, while others have a whorl of tube-like nectaries, as in the hellebores.

Stamens and ovaries (the male and female organs) are always numerous. The

ovaries, often arranged in a conical cluster, give rise to single-seeded, beaked nutlets called achenes, or to pods, known as follicles, that contain several seeds.

Most members of the family have acrid, poisonous sap that deters grazing animals. Monkshood is deadly and just handling the flower-spikes can cause palpitations. Extracts from this plant have been used to alleviate heart ailments and in homeopathic treatment of colds and chills.

Most of these plants are scarce in some localities and some, such as the pasqueflower, are rare. Pheasant's-eye, a once-common weed now almost extinct due to modern farming methods, is considered endangered.

◀ The Easter-blooming pasqueflower is restricted to a few warm, dry slopes in southern and eastern Britain.

▼ In early spring, wood anemone carpets ancient woods with its white blooms. A large colony can fill the air with its sharp, musky scent.

Wood anemone (windflower)
Anemone nemorosa

Blue anemone
Anemone apennina

Yellow anemone
Anemone ranunculoides

ANEMONES AND RELATIVES FACT FILE

● **Wood anemone (windflower)**
Anemone nemorosa
Habitat and distribution
Common in some deciduous woodlands, old hedgerows and pastures, and on mountain ledges
Size 10–30cm (4–12in) tall
Key features
Dainty perennial carpeting the ground in woods, with creeping stems; leaves fern-like, deeply lobed, in threes, stalked; flowers white, with 6–12 spreading petals, solitary, nodding in bud, 1cm (½in) across
Flowering time
March–May

● **Yellow anemone**
Anemone ranunculoides
Habitat and distribution
Occasionally naturalised in English woodlands
Size 10–20cm (4–8in) tall
Key features
Similar to wood anemone but leaves short-stalked; flowers yellow, solitary or paired, less than 1cm (½in) across
Flowering time
March–May

● **Blue anemone**
Anemone apennina
Habitat and distribution
Occasionally naturalised in English woodlands
Size 10–20cm (4–8in) tall
Key features
Similar to wood anemone but larger; flowers blue, 8–14 petals, downy underneath; fruit heads erect
Flowering time
March–April

● **Pasqueflower**
Pulsatilla vulgaris
Habitat and distribution
Rare, in short-cropped turf pastures on chalk and limestone slopes in southern and eastern England; strongholds in Cotswolds, Chilterns
Size 10–30cm (4–12in) tall
Key features
Tufted, silky haired perennial, dramatic-looking in flower; leaves feathery, twice-divided into deeply toothed lobes; large flowers rich violet purple, bell-shaped, solitary, with 6 petal-like sepals, 5–8cm (2–3in) across; fruit head of feathery plumed nutlets
Flowering time
April–May

● **Larkspur**
Consolida ajacis
Habitat and distribution
Rare, sporadic native weed of arable fields in East Anglia; also a garden escapee
Size 10–150cm (4–60in) tall
Key features
Erect, branched annual; leaves feathery, divided into numerous narrow, pointed segments; flowers blue (sometimes pink or white in garden escapees), with spreading petals and long spur, in long clusters, 1.5–2cm (⅝–¾in) across; fruit a solitary pod
Flowering time
June–August

Pasqueflower
Pulsatilla vulgaris

Larkspur
Consolida ajacis

A native of north-eastern Europe, the blue anemone is frequently planted for naturalising in orchards and wild gardens. It occasionally escapes and becomes naturalised in the wild.

ANEMONES AND RELATIVES FACT FILE

● **Winter aconite**
Eranthis hyemalis
Habitat and distribution
Widely naturalised in damp woodlands and
churchyards, mostly in eastern England
Size 5–15cm (2–6in) tall
Key features
Small perennial with a tuber at its base;
leaves deeply cut into narrow lobes, in whorl
of 3, forming ruff below flower; flowers
golden yellow, solitary, with 5–8 petals,
3–4cm (1¼–1½in) across; fruit a cluster of 5–8
small pods
Flowering time
January–March

● **Globeflower**
Trollius europaeus
Habitat and distribution
Damp meadows and stream sides in
upland Wales and northern Britain; also
north-western Ireland
Size 30–70cm (12–28in) tall
Key features
Tufted perennial similar to a large buttercup;
leaves deeply cut into 3–5 wedge-shaped,
much-divided and toothed lobes; flowers
lemon yellow, solitary, 3–5cm (1¼–2in) across,
with concave, rounded petals; fruit a cluster
of pods
Flowering time
May–August

● **Marsh-marigold (kingcup)**
Caltha palustris
Habitat and distribution
Marshes, ditches, damp meadows and
freshwater throughout British Isles, common
in some areas
Size 10–60cm (4–24in) tall
Key features
Tufted perennial similar to a large buttercup;
leaves shiny, toothed, kidney-shaped, long-
stalked; flowers glossy, golden yellow, 3–5cm
(1¼–2in) across; 5–8 petals (modified sepals),
in loose, leafy clusters; fruit a cluster of 5–15
beaked pods
Flowering time
May–July
Variety radicans more slender, creeping,
with smaller flowers made up of narrower
sepals, found by mountain streams

● **Stinking hellebore**
Helleborus foetidus
Habitat and distribution
In open woodlands and scrub on chalk and
limestone in parts of southern England, the
Welsh borders and eastern Wales; widely
naturalised elsewhere
Size 30–80cm (12–32in) tall
Key features
Sturdy, evergreen perennial with unpleasant
smell; leaves dark green, deeply cut into
9–11 spear-shaped, toothed lobes, all on the
stem; flowers bright yellow-green, purple-
edged, bell-shaped, 1–3cm (½–1¼in) across, in
drooping clusters; fruit a cluster of 3 pods
Flowering time
January–May

● **Green hellebore**
Helleborus viridis
Habitat and distribution
In open woodlands and on hedge-banks on
chalk and limestone in south-east England
and scattered sites north to Lancashire
Size 20–40cm (8–16in) tall
Key features
Similar to stinking hellebore but usually
shorter, leaves dying down in winter; leaves
paler green, with fewer, broader lobes,
usually two at base of stem; flowers green,
bowl-shaped, 4–5cm (1½–2in) across
Flowering time
February–April

● **Pheasant's-eye**
Adonis annua
Habitat and distribution
Once a widespread weed of
arable fields on chalk in
southern England, but today
virtually extinct there; appears
rarely, on bare ground
Size 10–40cm (4–16in) tall
Key features
Branched annual like a
tiny garden anemone;
leaves three times divided
into narrow, pointed, feathery
segments; flowers scarlet with a
black centre, 1.5–2.5cm
(⅝–1in) across; fruit an elongated
cylindrical cluster of small nutlets
Flowering time
June–July

● **Columbine**
Aquilegia vulgaris
Habitat and distribution
In damp woodlands, grassland and scrub on
lime-rich soils, in southern England; garden
escapees widespread elsewhere
Size 40–100cm (16–40in) tall
Key features
Tufted perennial; leaves twice divided into
oval, 2–3-lobed leaflets, mostly at base;
flowers blue, nodding, 2–3cm (1in) long, with
5 hooked spurs, in loose clusters; escapees
from gardens often have violet, pink or white
flowers and straighter spurs; fruit a cluster of
5 sticky, hairy pods
Flowering time
May–June

● **Monkshood**
Aconitum napellus
Habitat and distribution
Shaded stream banks and wet woodlands in
south-western Britain; sometimes naturalised
elsewhere
Size 50–150cm (20–60in) tall
Key features
Tall, erect, leafy perennial; leaves deeply cut
into wedge-shaped segments, each divided
into narrow, toothed lobes; flowers violet
blue, helmet-like, 2cm (1in) long, in
conspicuous spikes; fruit a cluster of 3 pods
Flowering time
May–September

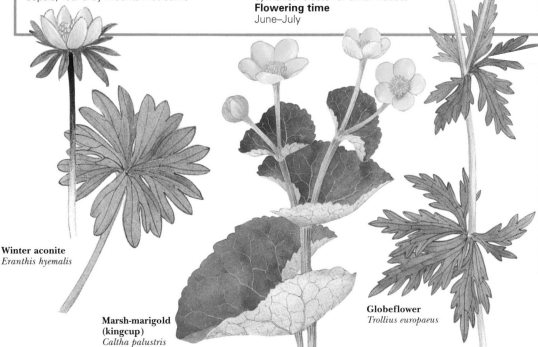

Winter aconite
Eranthis hyemalis

**Marsh-marigold
(kingcup)**
Caltha palustris

Globeflower
Trollius europaeus

The large, bright yellow petals
of the striking globeflower
bunch together in the manner of
a rose. Like most of its relatives,
it is very poisonous but is often
grown in gardens, including
forms with orange flowers.

Pheasant's-eye
Adonis annua

Monkshood is one of the most poisonous of all British plants – even skin contact can be dangerous. To see this fine plant growing truly wild, go to the West Country or the Welsh Marches.

Stinking hellebore
Helleborus foetidus

Green hellebore
Helleborus viridis

Columbine
Aquilegia vulgaris

Monkshood
Aconitum napellus

● **Common meadow-rue**
Thalictrum flavum
Habitat and distribution
Watersides, fens and wet meadows, mainly on lime-rich soils; rare in Scotland and Ireland
Size 20–100cm (8–40in) or more tall
Key features
Erect, sturdy, branched perennial; leaves divided two or three times into shallow-lobed or toothed leaflets; flowers feathery, erect, in compact clusters, with 12 or more upright yellow stamens; fruit a cluster of pods
Flowering time
June–August

● **Lesser meadow-rue**
Thalictrum minus
Habitat and distribution
Grassland, cliffs and rocks on limestone, mountain ledges, by shingle lakes and streams, and sand dunes; scarce in southern England; also widely naturalised
Size 25–100cm (10–40in) or more tall
Key features
Similar to common meadow-rue but often smaller; flowers 4 petalled, yellowish, often tinged purple, in loose clusters, long-stalked, drooping, with long, hanging, yellowish stamens; leaves divided into three or four leaflets that are mainly as broad as they are long
Flowering time
July–August

● **Alpine meadow-rue**
Thalictrum alpinum
Habitat and distribution
Ledges, damp rocks, grassland in mountains of northern Britain, Snowdonia and western Ireland
Size 5–15cm (2–6in) tall
Key features
Similar to common meadow-rue but much smaller, unbranched, leaves mostly at base; tiny flowers in loose, few-flowered clusters, drooping, with four purplish petals and about 10 long hanging, yellowish stamens
Flowering time
June–July

● **Baneberry (herb Christopher)**
Actaea spicata
Habitat and distribution
Damp ash woodlands and crevices of limestone pavements in northern England
Size 30–60cm (12–24in) tall
Key features
Unpleasant-smelling, erect perennial; leaves divided into oval, toothed leaflets; flowers white, feathery, in loose stalked spikes; fruit a spike of shiny, black berries
Flowering time
May–June

● **Mousetail**
Myosurus minimus
Habitat and distribution
A rare and decreasing plant of bare ground and damp hollows in arable fields in southern England, especially near the sea
Size 5–10cm (2–4in) tall
Key features
Low, hairless annual with slender leafless stems; leaves narrow, strap-shaped, in rosette at base; tiny flowers with greenish yellow sepals, solitary, 6–8mm (¼in) long; fruit a conspicuous cylindrical spike of tiny nutlets like the fruit of a small plantain
Flowering time
May–June

Once frequently found in damp arable fields, mousetail is now scarce and occurs in specific locations only. This small, inconspicuous plant favours the bare, moist ground alongside paths and around cattle troughs.

Mousetail
Myosurus minimus

Common meadow-rue
Thalictrum flavum

Alpine meadow-rue
Thalictrum alpinum

Lesser meadow-rue
Thalictrum minus

Baneberry or herb Christopher
Actaea spicata

WILDLIFE WATCH

Where do anemones and related plants grow?

● Anemones are mainly found in deciduous woodlands, often flowering well before the summer leaf canopy has developed.

● Common meadow-rue, globeflower, marsh-marigold and monkshood are plants of wet pastures or marshy places.

● Pasqueflower is a feature of some areas of unploughed chalk grassland in southern England.

● Mousetail grows in bare ground or damp fields, while pheasant's-eye is a rare weed of chalky arable fields.

Wild violets

Of the nine native species of violet, only one has the heady and much-loved scent. The suitably named sweet violet is a familiar sight in English country lanes, but less so elsewhere.

Ranging from small-flowered heartseases to the showy bedding pansies of public gardens, the genus *Viola* includes both pansies and violets. Britain's native violets all have small but distinctive flowers, usually

The strongly scented sweet violet is widespread in England, less so in Scotland, Wales and Ireland. Prolonged exposure to the scent will temporarily dull the sense of smell, making it doubly effective at covering up unpleasant odours.

violet, bluish or white in colour. They are distinguished from pansies by their smaller, inconspicuous stipules, which are paired leaf-like structures at the base of the leaf stalks. The stipules of violets are quite simple in form and sometimes toothed. Those of pansies are much more lobed, leafy and noticeable.

Violets are perennials, often with a rosette of long-stalked, heart-shaped, neatly toothed or scalloped leaves. Flowers are solitary on slender stalks and

actually hang upside-down, as the flower stalk bends sharply just below the flower. Each has five petals, arranged regularly, almost like a tiny face. The central and largest petal extends into a hollow spur, filled with the sweet nectar that attracts insect pollinators. Five male pollen-producing organs (stamens) are grouped around the female ovary in the centre of the flower.

At the end of the flowering season some species produce inconspicuous flowers that do

not open, but set seed by self-pollination. Violet seeds are attractive to ants, which gather and thus disperse them.

Heavenly fragrance

Sadly, not all violet flowers emit the well-known fragrant scent. To most people, especially country dwellers, the 'true' violet is sweet violet (*Viola odorata*). Its richly scented flowers are an early indicator of coming spring, and can be found on sheltered banks and beside lanes and in

◄ Found in woodlands and grasslands throughout Britain, the common dog violet flowers from late March to June.

▼ The marsh violet favours the mountain and moorland habitats of northern and western Britain and Ireland, growing in wet conditions, often alongside bog plants such as *Sphagnum* moss.

churchyards from late February or March onwards. In some areas, sweet violets with white flowers are more common than the purple-violet variety, although there are often plenty of those too, and flowers in various shades of purplish pink, lilac and even apricot or yellow are occasionally to be seen. The precise native distribution of the sweet violet is difficult to establish, as there has been so much migration from cottage gardens to the wild – and back again.

Ever popular

The sweet violet has a long history in medicine, with uses for both the leaves and the roots. In Greece, for example, an infusion of violets is still employed to treat bronchitis, and as a diuretic and gentle laxative. Elsewhere, sugar-crystallised flowers may be used to decorate a variety of cakes and chocolates.

Violets are the basis, too, of an ancient perfume industry on the French Riviera and are a familiar ingredient of soaps, bath-oils and perfumes.

Sweet violets were especially popular with the Victorians, who bred many garden forms. Today violets are still grown in the West Country for the early cut-flower trade. However, many of the larger cultivated flowers are scentless and the best violets are still the wild, sweet flowers of woodland and hedgerow.

GARDEN VIOLA

Also known as the horned pansy, *Viola cornuta*, to give it its scientific name, is a garden escapee, especially common in eastern Scotland. A perennial that spreads via slender, creeping underground stems, or rhizomes, it grows to about 30cm (12in) tall and has oval, pointed, bluntly toothed leaves that are hairy underneath. The flowers, which appear from June to July, are pale bluish violet or lilac with white on the lower petal and, unlike native species except the sweet violet, they have a pleasant fragrance.

WILD VIOLET FACT FILE

● Sweet violet
Viola odorata
Habitat and distribution
Woodland margins, scrub, hedge-banks and churchyards, often semi-wild in or near gardens; widespread in England, but rare elsewhere
Size Up to 15cm (6in) tall
Key features
Spreads by long, rooting runners; leaves in a basal rosette, heart-shaped, hairless or sparsely hairy; flowers fragrant, 12–18mm (½–¾in) long, deep violet or white with a lilac spur; occasionally purplish pink, lilac or yellowish
Flowering time
February–early May, and sometimes in autumn

● Hairy (or spur) violet
Viola hirta
Habitat and distribution
Grassland, scrub and woodland margins on chalk or limestone, occasionally on sand dunes; common in certain parts of south and east England, but scarce or rare elsewhere
Size Up to 10cm (4in) tall
Key features
Similar to sweet violet but without runners; leaves in a basal rosette, heart-shaped, with short hairs; flowers unscented, around 15mm (⅝in) long, pale violet
Flowering time
March–May, and sometimes in autumn

● Teesdale violet
Viola rupestris
Habitat and distribution
A rare plant of short turf and bare ground on limestone in Upper Teesdale and a few other places in northern England
Size Up to 4cm (1½in) tall when in flower, may reach 10cm (4in) when fruiting
Key features
Similar to the dog violets but downy all over, with smaller, rounder heart-shaped leaves and broader less distinctly toothed stipules; flowers 10–15mm (½in) long, bluish violet, the short spur pale violet; downy fruits especially distinguish it from the dog violets
Flowering time
May

● Common dog violet
Viola riviniana
Habitat and distribution
Generally the commonest violet throughout the British Isles; sometimes a weed in gardens; a plant of woodlands, hedgerows, heaths and coastal and mountain grassland
Size Up to 4cm (1½in) tall in flower, and 10cm (4in) tall when fruiting
Key features
Leaves mostly in a loose, flowerless rosette, heart-shaped; flowers 12–18mm (½–¾in) long, bluish violet, with a stout, upcurved, cream or very pale violet spur that distinguishes it from early dog violet; on heathland, especially on the coast, more compact, with smaller leaves and flowers (subsp. *minor*)
Flowering time
Late March–May, and sometimes in July–September

● Wood (or early) dog violet
Viola reichenbachiana
Habitat and distribution
Common in some woodlands and hedgerows in England, Wales and Ireland, usually in more shaded habitats and on richer soils than common dog violet
Size Up to 15cm (6in) tall
Key features
Leaves mostly in a loose, flowerless rosette, heart-shaped, more pointed and paler than those of common dog violet; flowers 12–18mm (½–¾in) long, violet, with a slender, straight, un-notched darker violet spur that distinguishes it from common dog-violet
Flowering time
March–April

● Heath dog (or heath) violet
Viola canina
Habitat and distribution
Widespread on dry and wet heaths, both inland and on coasts, and in fens
Size Up to 40cm (16in) tall
Key features
Leaves not in rosette, heart to spear-shaped, often rather thick, hairless; flowers 15–25mm (⅝–1in) long, pale blue, the spur yellowish green or whitish
Flowering time
Late April–June

V. canina* subsp. *montana is more erect, with narrower leaves and paler blue flowers; it is a rare plant of fens in Cambridgeshire and Huntingdonshire

● Pale dog (or pale heath) violet
Viola lactea
Habitat and distribution
A rare plant of damp coastal and inland heaths, mostly in south and south-west England, south and west Wales, and south-west Ireland
Size Up to 20cm (8in) tall
Key features
Leaves not in a rosette, slender; flowers 15–20mm (⅝–¾in) long, pale bluish white, the short spur greenish; the pale flowers distinguish this from the other violets except fen violet
Flowering time
May–June

● Fen violet
Viola persicifolia
Habitat and distribution
An extremely rare plant of grassy fens, reduced to a few sites in Cambridgeshire and one in Oxfordshire; also in a few turloughs, or temporary lakes, in western Ireland
Size Up to 30cm (12in) tall
Key features
Similar to pale dog violet but more upright and with creeping runners; leaves not in a basal rosette, narrowly triangular; flowers 10–15mm (½in) long, bluish white, veined violet, the very short spur greenish; the pale flowers distinguish this from other violets except heath dog violet; the short, roundish petals and the short spur are distinctive
Flowering time
May–June

● Marsh violet
Viola palustris
Habitat and distribution
Damp ground on acid (lime-poor) soil, especially peat-bogs; common in the north and west of Britain, and in much of Ireland, especially the west
Size Up to 10cm (4in) tall
Key features
Distinguished from other violets by the creeping underground stems or rhizomes; leaves broad, rounded to kidney-shaped, green, mostly hairless; stipules with few teeth; flowers 10–15mm (½in) long, pale blue or lilac, veined purple, the spur very short
Flowering time
April–July

V. palustris* subsp. *juressii has more pointed leaves with hairy stalks; widespread but less common

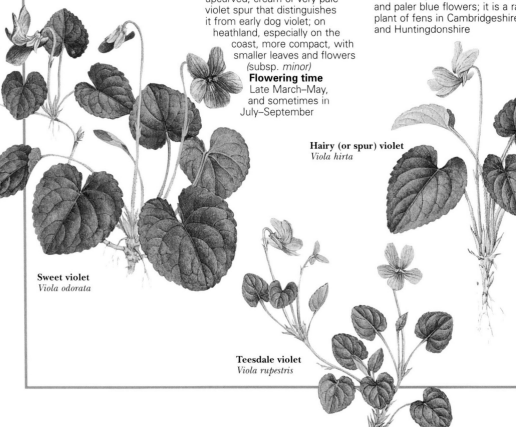

Sweet violet
Viola odorata

Hairy (or spur) violet
Viola hirta

Teesdale violet
Viola rupestris

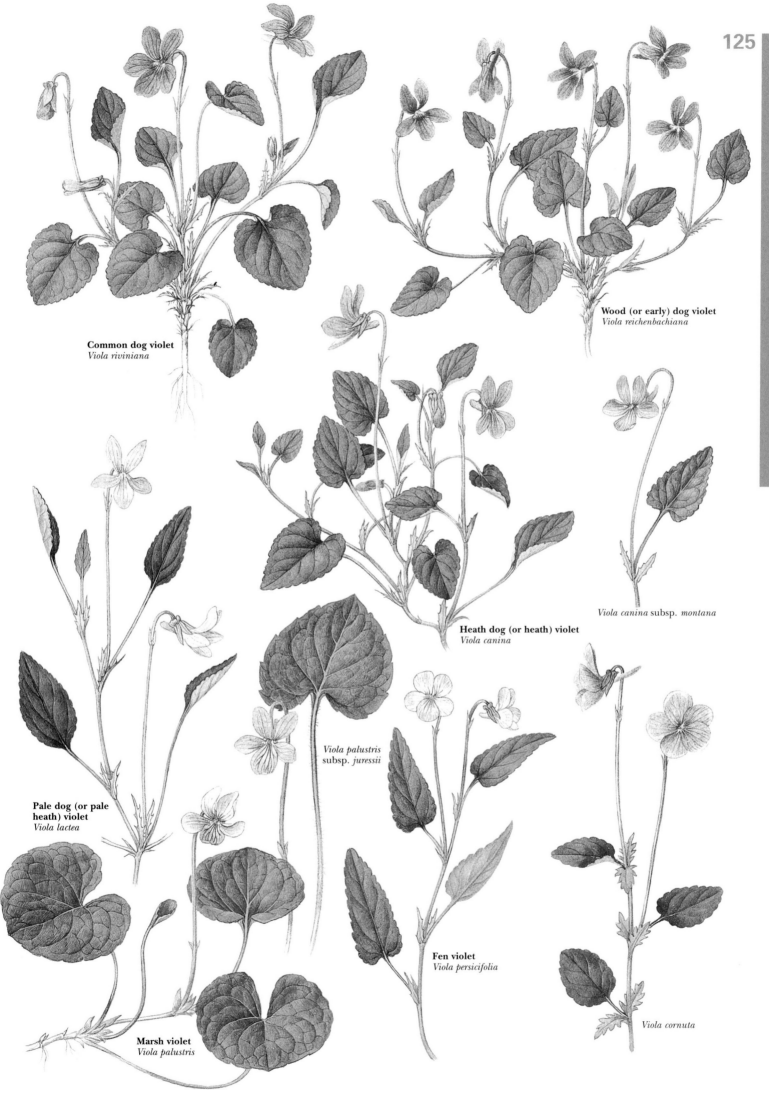

Common dog violet
Viola riviniana

Wood (or early) dog violet
Viola reichenbachiana

Heath dog (or heath) violet
Viola canina

Viola canina subsp. *montana*

Pale dog (or pale heath) violet
Viola lactea

Viola palustris
subsp. *juressii*

Marsh violet
Viola palustris

Fen violet
Viola persicifolia

Viola cornuta

Index

Page numbers in *italic* refer to
illustrations

A

aconite, winter (*Eranthis hyemalis*)
119, *119*
acorns *29*, 30, 33
adder 45
anemones 117–21
  blue (*Anemone apennina*) 118, *118*
  wood (*Anemone nemorosa*) 8, 30, *32*,
    35, 36, 37, 42, 117, *117*, 118, *118*
  yellow (*Anemone ranunculoides*)
    118, *118*
ants 14, *15*
argus, brown 17
ash trees 8, 18, 37, *38*, 42
asphodel, bog 43
autumn lady's-tresses 14
avens, water 41

B

badger (*Meles meles*) 31, 33, *37*, 38,
  52, 86–91, *86–91*
baneberry (*Actaea spicata*) 121, *121*
basil, wild 18–19
bats
  long-eared *30*, 31
  pipistrelle *30*
  whiskered *37*
Beachy Head 16
bedstraw, heath 42
beech trees 8, *8*, *12*, 22, 23, 37
bee-fly, common *37*
bellflower, clustered 13, *13*
bent
  common or fine (*Agrostis
    capillaris*) 78, *78*
  creeping (*Agrostis stolonifera*) 78, *78*
bilberry 43
birch trees 28, 38, 42
bird's-foot trefoil 13, 17
blackbird *22*, 27, 56
blackcap 9, 42
blackthorn 18, *20*
bloody-nosed beetle (*Timarcha
  tenebricosa*) 72, *72*
bluebell (*Hyacinthoides non-scripta*) 8,
  9, *28*, 30, 34–39, *34–39*, 42, 43
  Spanish *37*
blue butterflies 17
  adonis 17, *17*
  chalkhill 7, 17
  common 7, 17
  small 17
bog myrtle 43
Border Forest Park 45
Box Hill 16
bracken 43, 44
brambling (*Fringilla montifringilla*)
  104, 105, *105*, 106, *106*
brimstone butterfly *34*
brome, upright (*Bromopsis erecta*) 14,
  79, *79*
brown butterflies 17
  meadow 17
buckthorn 13
buff-tip moth *26*
bullfinch (*Pyrrhula pyrrhula*) 104,
  105, *105*, 109, *109*
buntings 66–70
  cirl (*Emberiza cirlus*) 66, 69, *69*
  corn (*Miliaria calandra*) *16*, 66,
    66, 70, *70*

Lapland (*Calcarius lapponicus*) 66,
  70, *70*
ortolan (*Emberiza hortulana*) 66,
  70, *70*
reed (*Emberiza schoeniclus*) 66, *66*,
  68, *68*
snow (*Plectrophenax nivalis*) 66, 68, *68*
burnet moths 17
Butser Hill 16
buttercups 117
butterflies 17
  see also individual types of butterfly
buzzard 52

C

caddis flies 45
campion, red *22*, 38–39
celandine, lesser 8, 36, *36*
centipedes 111–14, *112*
  brown *113*, *114*
  European house (*Scutigera
    coleoptrata*) 113, *114*
  scolopendromorph 113
  snake 112, 113, 114
chaffinch (*Fringilla coelebs*) 104, 105,
  105
chalk downlands 7, 12–17, *12–17*
chalk false-brome (*Brachypodium
  rupestre*) 79, *79*
chestnut 36, 38
chickweed wintergreen 42, 43
chiffchaff 9, 42
climate change 39
clover 53
cockchafer *9*
cock's-foot (*Dactylis glomerata*) 75,
  77, *77*
columbine (*Aquilegia vulgaris*) 117,
  119, *120*
Compton Down 16
conifers 43
coppices 21, 36–37, *38*
cord-grass, common (*Spartina
  anglica*) 76, *76*
cornel, dwarf 43
cottongrass 43
couch grass, sand (*Elytrigia juncea*)
  76, *76*
cowberry 43
cow parsley *22*, 39
cowslip 7
cranberry 43
cranefly *32*
crane's-bill, wood 43, *43*
crested dog's tail (*Cynosurus
  cristatus*) 77, *77*
crested hair grass 14
crossbill (*Loxia curvirostra*) 43, *43*,
  104, *105*, 110, *110*
crowberry 43
cuckoo *6*
cuckoo flower *9*, 115
curlew *40*, 44

D

daffodils 8
daisy, ox-eye 13, *13*
dandelions (*Taraxacum officinale*)
  80–81, *80–81*
  common 81, *81*
  lesser 81, *81*
  narrow-leaved marsh 80, 81, *81*
  red-veined 81, *81*
dawn chorus 31

deer 30
deergrass 43
Devil's Dyke 16
dipper 45
dog's mercury 7, 35
dogwood 13, 38
dor beetles
  common (*Geotrupes stercorarius*)
    71, *71*, 72, *72*, 73, *74*
  wood (*Geotrupes stercorosus*) 72
dormouse 24, 26, 30, 37, 38, 56
downlands 7, 12–17, *12–17*
drinker moth 17, *17*
dryad's saddle *33*
Duke of Burgundy 8, 17
dumbledor (*Geotrupes stercorarius*)
  71, *71*, 72
dung beetles (*Aphodius, Geotrupes*)
  71–74, *71–74*
  horned (*Copris lunaris*) 74
dunlin 44
Dutch elm disease 18

E

eggar moth, northern 45
elm 18
emperor moth 45
epiphytes 38

F

ferns 30, 38
fescue 53
  red or creeping (*Festuca rubra*) 14,
    75, 78, *78*
  sheep's (*Festuca ovina*) 14, 78, *78*
fieldfare 27
finches 9, 27, 66, 104–10, *104–10*
fleas 50
flies 71
flycatcher, pied 31, 42
fox 22, 33, 52, 54, 59, 92–97, *92–97*
fox moth 45
foxtail, meadow (*Alopecurus
  pratensis*) 77, *77*
fritillary, snakeshead 7
fritillary butterflies 38
  dark green 17, *17*
  silver-washed *32*
fungi 33, 39

G

galls 31–32
  knopper 32
  marble 32
  oak apple *29*, 31–32
  spangle *29*
gall wasp *29*, 37
gentian, autumn 13
'ghost hedges' 18
Glastonbury thorn 26
global warming 39
globeflower (*Trollius europaeus*) 41,
  119, *119*, 121
glow-worms 15
goldcrest 33
goldfinch (*Carduelis carduelis*) 104,
  105, *105*, 107, *107*
goosander 45
gorse 18, 44
goshawk 43, *43*
grasses 13, 75–79, *75–79*
grasshoppers 14
  rufous 14

stripe-winged 14, *14*
grasslands 7, 12–17, *12–13*, *16–17*, 75
Grasslees Burn Wood 45
grass moths 17
grass-of-Parnassus 41, *41*
greenfinch (*Carduelis chloris*) 104,
  105, *105*, 106, *106*
grouse
  black 44
  red 44
gull, great black-backed 52–53

H

Hadrian's Wall 40, *41*, 42, 45
hairstreak, purple 31
Harbottle Crags 45
hare, brown *6*
harebell 13, 34
harestail 43
hawfinch (*Coccothraustes
  coccothraustes*) 27, *27*, 104, *105*,
  110, *110*
hawkbit
  autumnal 13
  rough 13
hawk's-beards 80, 82
  beaked (*Crepis vesicaria*) 82, *83*
  bristly (*Crepis setosa*) 82, *83*
  marsh (*Crepis paludosa*) 82, *82*
  northern or soft (*Crepis mollis*) 82,
    83
  rough (*Crepis biennis*) 82, *83*
  smooth (*Crepis capillaris*) 82, *82*
  stinking (*Crepis foetida*) 82, *82*
hawkweeds 80, 84
  alpine (*Hieracium holosericeum*) 84,
    84
  mouse-ear (*Pilosella officinarum*)
    13, 84, *84*
  narrow-leaved (*Hieracium
    umbellatum*) 84, *84*
hawthorn 13, 18, 38
  common (*Crataegus monogyna*)
    24–27, *24–27*
  Midland (*Crataegus laevigata*) 25,
    25
hazel 18, 36, 38, *38*, 42
heartsease 122
heath butterfly, small 17, 45
heather 44–45
  bell 40, *40*, 43
  common 40
hedgerows 9, 18–23, *18–23*
hellebores 117
  green (*Helleborus viridis*) 119, *120*
  stinking (*Helleborus foetidus*) 119, *120*
herb Christopher (*Actaea spicata*)
  121, *121*
Hieracium
  acuminatum 84
  anglicum 84
  britannicum 84
  caledonicum 84
  decolor 84
  dewarii 84
  latobrigorum 84
  lingulatum 84
  orcadense 84
  prenanthoides 84
  sabaudum 84
  trichocaulon 84
  vulgatum 84
hobby 15
holly 18, *18*, 38
Holystone Woodlands 45

honeydew 14
honeysuckle 38
Hooper's Rule, hedges 23

I

Ivinghoe Beacon 16
ivy 23, 38

J

jay *30*, 33

K

kestrel 15, *15*, 44
Kielder Forest 43
kingcup (*Caltha palustris*) 119, *119*
knapweed 13, 17

L

lackey moth 26
lady's bedstraw 14
Lamyctes fulvicornis 113
lappet moth 26, *26*
lapwing 44
larkspur (*Consolida ajacis*) 118, *118*
laying hedges 21, *21*, 24, 26
lichen 38, 42
lime, small-leaved 18
ling 40, 43
linnet (*Carduelis cannabina*) 104,
    105, *105*, 109, *109*
lithobiomorphs 113
Lithobius 114
    variegatus 113
lizard, common 45
lousy watchman 72

M

magpie 27
maples 18, 38
marbled white butterfly 17
mare's-tail 45
marjoram 13
marram grass (*Ammophila arenaria*)
    75, 76, *76*
marsh-marigold (*Caltha palustris*)
    44, 45, 119, *119*, 121
maybug *9*
mayflies 45
may tree *see* hawthorn
meadow cat's-tail (*Phleum pratense*)
    76, *76*
meadow grass
    rough (*Poa trivialis*) 79, *79*
    sea (*Puccinellia maritima* 76, *76*
    smooth (*Poa pratensis*) 79, *79*
meadow-rue
    alpine (*Thalictrum alpinum*) 121, *121*
    common (*Thalictrum flavum*) 121,
        121
    lesser (*Thalictrum minus*) 121, *121*
meadows 75, *75*
meadowsweet 45
merlin 43, 44
mice
    wood *24*, 27, 33, 38, 54
    yellow-necked 37
milkwort 42
millipedes 39, 111–14
    flat-backed 113, *113*
    pill *111*, 112, 113
    red-striped snake *114*
    snake 112, *112*, 113, *113*, 114
minotaur beetle (*Typhaeus typhoeus*)
    73–74, *73*
monkshood (*Aconitum napellus*) 117,
    119, *120*, 121
moorland 42–43, 44
morel fungi *36*, 39

mosquitoes 50
mosses 30, 38, 42
moths 17, 31
mousetail (*Myosurus minimus*) 121, *121*
Muckle Moss 45
mushrooms 33
myxomatosis 13, 50–51

N

nightingale 9, 38
Northumberland 40–45, *40–45*
nuthatch 32, 33, 38

O

oak eggar moth 26
oak galls *see* galls
oaks 7, *12*, 18, 28–33, *28–33*, 35–37, *38*
    holm 29
    pedunculate, common or English
        (*Quercus robur*) 28, 29, *29*, 30, 32
    red 29
    sessile or durmast (*Quercus
        petraea*) 28, 29, *29*, 42, *42*
    Turkey 29, 32
oat-grass
    false (*Arrhenatherum elatius*) 77, *77*
    meadow (*Helictotrichon pratense*)
        14, 78, *78*
Onthophagus 73
    coenobita 73
orange-tip butterfly *32*, 115–16,
    115–16
orchids 14, *14*
    bee 14, *14*
    burnt *14*
    early purple *6*, 30, 37
    frog 14
    heath spotted 43
    lesser twayblade 43
    monkey 14, *14*
    musk 14
    pyramidal *14*
otter 45
ouzel, ring 44
owls 33, 52
    barn (*Tyto alba*) 59, 60–65, *60–65*
    short-eared 43, 44
    tawny *35*, 59

P

pasqueflower (*Pulsatilla vulgaris*) 13,
    13, 117, *117*, 118, *118*, 121
Pennine Way 45
peregrine 44
pheasant's-eye (*Adonis annua*) 117,
    119, *120*, 121
pine marten 43, *43*, 59
pines 28, 43
    Scots 18
pipit, meadow 15, 43, 44
plover, golden 44
pollarded trees 20
primrose 9, 18, *20*, 30, 37, *39*
pug moth, common 26
Pulpit Hill 16

Q

quaking grass (*Briza media*) 14, 78, *78*

R

rabbit (*Oryctolagus cuniculus*) 9, *12*,
    13, 30, 48–53
rabbit haemorrhagic disease 51
ragged-robin 41
redpoll (*Carduelis flammea*) 104,
    105, *105*, 108, *108*
redshank 44
redstart 42, *42*

redwing 27
reed canary grass (*Phalaris
    arundinacea*) 76, *76*
rice-grass (*Spartina anglica*) 76, *76*
robin 9, 27, 42
rock-rose, common 14
roe deer 27, *31*, 33, 43
roseroot 41, *41*
rowan 42
ryegrass, perennial (*Lolium perenne*)
    75, 77, *77*

S

St John's-wort, perforate *18–19*
salad burnet 14
salmon *44*, 45
saltmarsh grass, common
    (*Puccinellia maritima*) 76, *76*
sand twitch grass (*Elytrigia juncea*)
    76, *76*
saw-wort, alpine 41
saxifrages
    mossy 41
    starry 41
scabious 13, 17
scarab beetles 73
    English (*Copris lunaris*) 73, 74
sea poa (*Puccinellia maritima*) 76, *76*
sedges 14, 30
shardborne (*Geotrupes stercorarius*)
    71, *71*, 72
shaws 22
sheep 13, *13*, 16, 40, 42
shoveler *44*, 45
shrews 37
siskin (*Carduelis spinus*) 104, 105,
    105, 107, *107*
skippers 17
    dingy 17, *17*
    Essex 17
    grizzled 17
    large 17
    Lulworth 17
    silver-spotted 17
    small 17
skylark 14–15, *15*
snails 15, *15*
    dark-lipped 15
    Roman or edible 15, *15*
    round-mouthed 15, *15*
    white-lipped 15
snipe 44
snowdrop 8
sorrel, wood *33*
sparrowhawk *38*
speckled wood butterfly 38
Sphagnum moss 43
spruces 43
spurge, wood *28*, 37
squirrels 27
    grey *22*, *31*, 33
    red 43, *43*
stag beetle 28, *32*
stitchwort, greater 37
stoat 52, 59
stoneflies 45
sundew, round-leaved 43
swan, whooper 45, *45*

T

Therfield Heath 16
thistles
    dwarf 13, *13*
    melancholy 41
thrushes 27, 56
    mistle 27
    song 9, 42
thyme, wild 14
timothy grass (*Phleum pratense*) 76,
    76
tits 33, 37–38

blue 31
    great 31, 32
    long-tailed *24*, 27
toadstools 33
tor grass (*Brachypodium rupestre*) 79,
    79
tormentil 42
totter grass (*Briza media*) 14, 78, *78*
traveller's joy 23
treecreeper 33, 38
trout 45
twite (*Carduelis flavirostris*) 104, 105,
    105, 108, *108*

V

vernal grass, sweet (*Anthoxanthum
    odoratum*) 77, *77*
vetches
    horseshoe 13, 53
    kidney 13
Viola 122–5, *122–5*
    canina subsp. *montana* 124, *125*
    cornuta 123, *125*
    palustris subsp. *juressii* 124, *125*
violets *20*, 122–5, *122–5*
    common dog (*Viola riviniana*) *36*,
        123, 124, *125*
    fen (*Viola persicifolia*) 124, *125*
    hairy (*Viola hirta*) 124, *124*
    heath dog (*Viola canina*) 124, *125*
    marsh (*Viola palustris*) *123*, 124,
        125
    pale dog (*Viola lactea*) 124, *125*
    sweet (*Viola odorata*) 122–3, *122*,
        124, *124*
    Teesdale (*Viola rupestris*) 124, *124*
    wood dog (*Viola reichenbachiana*)
        124, *125*
voles 15, 33, *63*
    bank (*Clethrionomys glareolus*) 22,
        26, 27, 37, 38, *39*, 54–59, *54–59*
    field 44, 54
    Skomer 58, *58*

W

waders 44
wagtail, grey 45
warblers 37–38
    willow 42
    wood 42, *42*
weasel *9*, 33, 52, 59
wheatear 15, 44
whinchat 15
white admiral *33*, 38
wigeon *44*, 45
wild service tree 18
willowherb, alpine 41, *41*
windflower (*Anemone nemorosa*) 118,
    118
woodcock 38–39, *39*
woodlands 7–9, 28–39, *28–39*
woodlice 39, 112
woodpeckers
    great spotted (*Dendrocopos major*)
        30, 38,
        98–103, *98–103*
    green *8*
    lesser spotted 101, *101*
woodpigeon 27, *27*
woodruff 43
wren 33, 42
wryneck (*Jynx torquilla*) 103, *103*

Y

yellowhammer (*Emberiza citrinella*)
    15, *15*,
    66, 69, *69*
yellowtail moth *26*

Acknowledgments

Photographs: Front cover Woodfall Wild Images, inset OSF/I West; Back cover Mike Read; 1 OSF/I West; 2-3 NPL/William Osborn; 4 BC; 5 (t) Mike Read, (b) FLPA/W Wisniewski; 6 (all pics) NP; 7(bl) NP/Paul Sterry, (bc) NP/P Newman, (br) NP; 8(bl) NP/NA Callow, (bc) NP/EA Janes, (br) NP; 9(bl,bc) NP/Paul Sterry, (br) NP/O Newman; 10-11 NHPA/Andy Rouse; 12-13(b) NV/Heather Angel, 12(tr) NP/C Carver; 13(tr,cl,bl) Michael Chinery, (c, cr) NV/Heather Angel; 14(tr,br) Michael Chinery, (c,bl,bc) NV/Heather Angel; 15(tl,tr,cr) NP, (bl) NV/Jason Venus, (br) NV/G Moon; (bru) NHPA/EA Janes; 16(tl) NP/Paul Sterry, 16-17(b) NV/Heather Angel; 17(tr) Ardea/Ian Beames, (c) Ardea/J Bailey, (cr) NP/Paul Sterry; 18(bl) FLPA/EP Lawrence; 18-19 WW/Bob Gibbons; 20(tl) BC/P Hinchcliffe, (cr) BC/P Clement; 20-21(b) NV/Heather Angel, 21(tr) BC; (cl) NP/Paul Sterry, (cr) WW/M Hamblin; 22(tl) NPL, (tr) FLPA, (c) NHPA/Laurie Campbell, (br) NP/B Burbidge; 23(b) NHPA/Guy Edwardes; 24(cr) NHPA/EA Janes, (bl) NHPA/Stephen Dalton, (br) OSF; 24-25 NHPA/A Williams, 25(bl) WW/Bob Gibbons, (br) WW/David Woodfall; 26(tl) NHPA/EA Janes, (tr) WW/Bob Gibbons, (bl) WW/A Newman, (blu) NP/Paul Sterry, (br) NHPA/R Thompson; 27(tl) NP/J Russell, (tr) Ardea/D Avon, (b) NHPA/J Meech; 28-29 NV/Heather Angel; 29(bl) Mike Read, (bc) NP/Paul Sterry, (br) NP/Iris Bowen; 30(tl) NP/Hugh Clark, (c) Mike Read, (cr) NP/Paul Sterry; 30-31(b) Mike Read; 31(tl) Mike Read, (cl) NP/Owen Newman, (cr) NP/Colin Carver, (br) NV/Geoffrey Kings; 32(t) Mike Read, (tl) NP, (c) NP/Paul Sterry, (bru) NP/Paul Sterry, (br) Pat Morris; 33(t) NP/Paul Sterry, (br) Mike Read; 34(cl) NV/Heather Angel, (bc) OSF/K Porter, 34-35(b) NV/Heather Angel; 35(cr) Frank Blackburn; (br) OSF/M Wilding; 36(tl) Frank Blackburn, (c) OSF/Bob Gibbons, 36-37(b) Aquila; 37(tl) Garden Picture Library, (tr) OSF, (cr) OSF, (br) Dr P Elliot; 38(tc) Frank Blackburn, 38-39(t) Frank Blackburn; 39(cl) NV/Heather Angel, (cr,br) Frank Blackburn; 40(cl) OSF/GI Bernard, (bl) WW/M Powers, (br) WW/P Hicks; 41(sp) OSF/C Sharp, (cr) OSF/N Benvie, (bl) OSF/Bob Gibbons, (br) PW; 42(l) WW/David Woodfall, (tc) Windrush/David Tipling, (cr) Windrush/C Carver; 43(tl) OSF/T Tilford, (tr) WW/T Rasenen, (cl) WW/M McIntyre, (cr) Windrush/R Revels, (br) WW/David Woodfall; 44(tl) Windrush/David Tipling, (tr) OSF/C Sharp, (cl) NV/Heather Angel, (b) WW/David Woodfall, (b inset) WW/S Austin; 45(br) FLPA/W Wisniewski; 46-47 NHPA/Laurie Campbell; 48 BC; 49(tr) FLPA/Silvestris, BC/WS Paton; 50 BC; 51(tl) FLPA/F Merlet, (tr) NHPA/Michael Leach; 52(t) NPL, (bl) BC/Bob Glover; 53(t) FLPA/Chris Newton; 54 FLPA/G Laci, 55(tr) OSF/Ian West, (b) BC/P Clement; 56(cl) OSF/D Boag; 57(t) OSF/R Jackman, (bl) FLPA/R Bird, (br) FLPA/HD Brandl; 59(tr) FLPA/Silvestris, (br) OSF/Michael Leach; 59(tl) FLPA/Roger Wilmhurst, (tr) OSF/R Redfern; 60(b) NHPA/Stephen Dalton; 61 Mike Read; 62(tl) NHPA/Alan Williams, (cr) Mike Read; 63(l) NHPA/EA Janes; 64(tr) Mike Read, (bl) BC/Hans Reinhard; 65(tl,tc) Mike Read, (tr) NHPA/Tony Sauvenet, (cl) NV/Jason Venus, (c,cr) BC/Kim Taylor; 66-70 NP; 71(t) NP/SC Bisserot, (b) OSF; 72(t) PW, (bl) NP/D Smith, (br) Aquila/GW Ward; 73(tr,cl) NI/Bob Gibbons, (b) FLPA/G Hyde; 74(t) NI/Bob Gibbons, (bl) Aquila/D Meredith; 75(l) OSF/B Osborn, (r) OSF/GI Bernard; 76(bl) NV/Heather Angel, 77 PW; 78(tl) FLPA/I Rose, (br) NI/Bob Gibbons; 79(cr) PW; 80, 81, 83 (tl) NV/Heather Angel, 83 (br) Ardea/B. Gibbons; 85 NHPA/Stephen Dalton; 86, 87 OSF/Mark Hamblin; 88(cl) Mike Read, (br) NP; 89(tr) OSF/Robin Redfern, (cl,bc) FLPA/Martin B Withers; 90(t) FLPA/Martin B Withers; 91(tl) FLPA/F Merlet, (tr) OSF/Richard Packwood; (cr) FLPA/Roger Wilmhurst; 92 NHPA/A Rouse; 93(tr, cl) OSF/GI Bernard, (br) Ardea/E Dragesco; 94(b) OSF/T Heathcote, 95(tl) FLPA/T Whittaker, (tr) OSF/GI Bernard, (br) Ardea/S Meyers; 96(tr) OSF/I West, (bl) Ardea/M Watson; 97(t) OSF/Ian West, (b) Ardea/J Daniels; 98 NHPA/Stephen Dalton; 99(tr) BC/Kim Taylor, (bl) NP/Paul Sterry; 100(bc) NP/H Clark, (br) BC/Jane Burton; 101(tc) NPL/D Kjaer, (cr) OSF/A Anderson, (bl) NP/Hugh Clark, (br) BC/Jane Burton; 102(tl) NP/Paul Sterry, (cl) BC/J Jurkam (c) NP/Hugh Clark, (cr) NHPA/A Rouse, (bl) Mike Read, (bc) BC/D Green, (br) NHPA/R Tidman; 103(tl) Mike Read, (tr) NP/B Hughes, (b) NHPA/Laurie Campbell; 104 NPL;105(bl) NP/B Hughes; 106(tl) OSF/D Tipling; 107(cl,bl) NP/Paul Sterry; 108(tl) Windrush/D Tipling, (bl) NPL; 109(tl) FLPA/D Middleton, (bl) NP/Paul Sterry; 110(tl) Mike Read, (bl) OSF/M Leach; 111 NP/Paul Sterry; 112(tl,c) NP/Paul Sterry, (br) PW; 113(tr,br) PW, (bl) NP/Paul Sterry; 114(tr,c) PW, (b) NP/Paul Sterry; 115(tr) BC/Kim Taylor, (bl) NP/C Carver; 116(tl) NP/N Phelps, (tr) FLPA/I Rose, (bc) FLPA/P Head, (br) FLPA/GE Hyde; 117(c) NHPA/EA Janes, (b) NHPA/J Olsen/R Sorensen; 118(br) FLPA/I Rose; 119(br) A Gagg; 120(t) Garden Matters/John Feltwell; 121(tr) PW; 122 FLPA/W Wisniewski; 123(t) NP, (br) NP/Brinsley Burbidge.

Illustrations: 25, 76-84, 118-121, 124-125 Ian Garrard; 38 Ian Pritchard; 50-53, 56-59, 62-63, 88, 91, 94, 96, 100 John Ridyard; 93 Clive Pritchard; 105-110 Tim Hayward.

Key to Photo Library Abbreviations: BC = Bruce Coleman Ltd, FLPA = Frank Lane Photo Agency, GPL = Garden Picture Library; NHPA = Natural History Photo Agency, NI= Natural Image, NP = Nature Photographers, NPL = Nature Picture Library, NS = Natural Science Photos, NV = Heather Angel/Natural Visions, OSF = Oxford Scientific Films, PW = Premaphotos Wildlife, WW = Woodfall Wild.

Key to position abbreviations: b = bottom, bl = bottom left, blu = bottom left upper, br = bottom right, bru = bottom right upper, c = centre, cl = centre left, clu = centre left upper, cr = centre right, cru = centre right upper, l = left, r = right, sp = spread, t = top, tl = top left, tlu = top left upper, tr = top right, tru = top right upper.

Wildlife Watch
Grassland & Woodland in Spring

Published by the Reader's Digest Association Limited, 2004

The Reader's Digest Association Limited
11 Westferry Circus, Canary Wharf
London E14 4HE
www.readersdigest.co.uk

Reprinted 2004

We are committed to both the quality of our products and the service we provide to our customers, so please feel free to contact us on 08705 113366, or by email at: cust_service@readersdigest.co.uk

If you have any comments about the content of our books you can contact us at: gbeditorial@readersdigest.co.uk

® Reader's Digest, The Digest and the Pegasus logo are registered trademarks of The Reader's Digest Association, Inc., of Pleasantville, New York, USA

For Reader's Digest:
Series Editor Christine Noble
Project Art Editor Jane McKenna

Reader's Digest General Books:
Editorial Director Cortina Butler
Art Director Nick Clark

This book was designed, edited and produced by Eaglemoss Publications Ltd, based on material first published as the partwork *Wildlife of Britain*

For Eaglemoss:
Editors Marion Paull, Giles Sparrow
Art Editor Phil Gibbs
Consultant Jonathan Elphick
Publishing Manager Nina Hathway

Copyright © Eaglemoss Publications Ltd/Midsummer Books Ltd 2004

Printed and bound in Europe by Arvato Iberia

CONCEPT CODE: UK 0133/G/S
BOOK CODE: 630-003-2
ISBN: 0 276 42883 8
ORACLE CODE: 356200003H